Delusions

Excerpts from 5 STAR reviews on Amazon Kindle
DELUSIONS—Pragmatic Realism

...Stanislaw Kapuscinski spares nothing as he opens your mind to new thoughts and possibilities. ... His grasp of both science and religion is staggering and never ceases to impress me... This intelligent examination will leave you contemplating your own beliefs and place in the world for some time.
It is a gift and I highly recommend it!
(Ally McMahon, USA)

Stanislaw Kapuscinski... is not convinced by the dogmas of either religion or science, and he does a wonderful job of discussing both sides of this often intractable debate.
(John Allan. USA)

Kapuscinski's intentions are early implied, to match (R.) Dawkins bite for bite and (as honestly) to demonstrate the irreconcilable gulf between intellectual reductionism and emotional religious dogmatism... ...he takes on Dawkins full square and very gently gradually knocks him over. Not by a deft left hook, but by tugging at his shirt.
What remains is a deeply humane appeal to reap the best of human inspiration, devoid of dogma, restoring, indeed pleading for, worshipful sanity derived from self-knowledge and true identity.
I thought it brilliant.
(Philippa Rees, UK)

Opened my mind to a new way of thinking,
(J. Linson, USA)

Every now and then you come across a book you wished you had read years ago. "DELUSIONS - Pragmatic Realism" is one of these books.
Johann David Renner (Australia)

Other books by Stanislaw Kapuscinski

DICTIONARY OF BIBLICAL SYMBOLISM
KEY TO IMMORTALITY
VISULIZATION—Creating your own Universe
BEYOND RELIGION Volumes I
BEYOND RELIGION Volumes II
BEYOND RELIGION Volumes III
[Three Collections of Essays on Perception of Reality]

Fiction by Stan I.S. Law
(aka **Stanislaw Kapuscinski**)

Novels

WALL—Love, Sex, and Immortality [Aquarius Trilogy Book One]
PLUTO EFFECT [Aquarius Trilogy Book Two]
OLYMPUS—Of Gods and Men [Aquarius Trilogy Book Three]
YESHUA—Missing Years of Jesus
PETER AND PAUL—Intuitive Sequel to Yeshûa
MARVIN CLARK—In Search of Freedom
GIFT OF GAMMAN
ENIGMA OF THE SECOND COMING
ONE JUST MAN [Winston Trilogy Book One]
ELOHIM [Winston Trilogy Book Two]
WINSTON'S KINGDOM [Winston Trilogy Book Three]
THE PRINCESS
GATE—Things my Mother told Me
ALEC [Alexander Trilogy Book One]
ALEXANDER [Alexander Trilogy Book Two]
SACHA—THE WAY BACK [Alexander Trilogy Book Three]
THE AVATAR SYNDROME [Prequel to the Headless World]
HEADLESS WORLD [Sequel to the Avatar Syndrome]
NOW—BEING AND BECOMING

Short stories

THE JEWEL AND OTHER SHORT STORIES
Sci-Fi Series 1
Sci-Fi Series 2
Cats & Dogs Series

DELUSIONS
Pragmatic Realism

Stanisław Kapuściński

INHOUSEPRESS, MONTREAL, CANADA

Copyright © Stanislaw Kapuscinski 1997
Ebook Edition March 04, 2012
Paperback Edition 2014
http://stanlaw.ca

All rights reserved. No part of this publication may be reproduced, stored in a retrieval system or transmitted in any form, or by any means electronic, mechanical, photocopying, recording or otherwise, without the prior written permission of the publisher.

Published by
INHOUSEPRESS
1470 St–Jacques, suite 7, Montreal, Qc., H3C 4J4

Design and layout
Bozena Happach

ISBN 978-0-9813015-2-5

Paperback Edition 2014
INHOUSEPRESS

Dedication

Dedicated to Richard Dawkins, in gratitude for many hours of enjoyable reading. While he and I don't always see eye to eye, he might find, here, additional arguments for his Cause Célèbre

Contents

FOREWORD   9
INTRODUCTION   11

PART ONE — PAST
Chapter 1. Fundamentalism in Religion and Science.   23
Chapter 2. Where We Were   30
Chapter 3. What We Were   35
Chapter 4. The God Diffusion   43
Chapter 5. The Beginning and the End.   53
Chapter 6. Why We Where: Phase One   59
Chapter 7. Atheist's Delusion.   63

PART TWO — PRESENT
Chapter 8. Fundamentalism in Religion and Science   71
Chapter 9. Where We Are   80
Chapter 10. What We Are   85
Chapter 11. The God Diffusion   95
Chapter 12. The End of the Beginning   105
Chapter 13. Why We Are: Phase Two   119
Chapter 14. Atheist's Delusion   129

PART THREE — FUTURE
Chapter 15. Fundamentalism in Religion and Science   139
Chapter 16. Where We Might Be   151
Chapter 17. What We Might Be   157
Chapter 18. The God Diffusion   165
Chapter 19. The Beginning of the End   174
Chapter 20. Why We Shall Be: Phase Three   181
Chapter 21. Scientist's Delusion   191

POSTSCRIPTUM   207

APPENDIX I — The Church   215
APPENDIX II — Science   220
APPENDIX III — Richard Dawkins   225

EPILOGUE   235

BIBLIOGRAPHY   238

FOREWORD

I am reminded of a story about a seeker, a man from the West, coming upon two Buddhist monks. They were sitting in a contemplative silence, some distance apart. After waiting for a respectful while, in an attempt to understand the Infinite, the tourist asked the first monk,
"Is there a God?"

The monk opened his eyes, looked with patient tolerance at the traveler and replied, "Of course not."

The seeker shook his head in deep disappointment. Yet, the scientific part of his brain smiled with satisfaction. On the other hand, having been trained in the scientific method he felt a deep void in his heart. His upbringing and training precluded the existence of the permanent; of something he could fall back on if all else failed, and in science things changed constantly—even the universe. But, he was a seeker; he refused to give up. After another while he approached the second monk and repeated the same question,
"Is there a God?"

The second monk opened his eyes, looked at the traveler with inherent compassion and replied, "Of course. I am."

It sounded like a Zen Koan. Or, in Master Hyakujo's words, "The enlightened man is *one* with causation."

The seeker remembered: "The perceiver and the perceived are one."

Contented, the seeker went on his way.

***

INTRODUCTION

*In nature there are neither rewards nor punishments;
there are consequences.*

Robert Green Ingersoll
American social activist, orator and agnostic (1833—1899)

As you must have gathered, or suspected from the dedication, this book has been inspired by Richard Dawkins's last book, *God Delusion*, or at least the last book of his I read. And this in spite of the fact that my hero seems quite unable to understand that in the USA, and probably in most other parts of the world, religions, for the most part, have nothing to do with the existence of god, only with political expediency. His determined, if justified, attacks on most religions, made me think that, after all, there is little difference between religion and science. I know he'd vehemently object to this sentiment, but so would all people who deeply believe in the righteousness of their cause. And don't be mistaken. With the author of *God Delusion*, the destruction of all things that most people hold holy is a cause. A *Cause Célèbre*.

Yet, one of many reasons why I admire Richard Dawkins is his inherent honesty. Having spent a good part of his book doing his damnedest to destroy religions, and even faith as such, he offers us the following statement:

> King James Bible of 1611—the Authorized Version—
> includes passages of outstanding literary merit in its own

right... (examples follow). But the main reason the English Bible needs to be part of our education is that it is a major source book for literary culture. The same applies to the legends of the Greek and Roman gods...

Such sentiment is rare indeed, and very close to my heart. I would add to this selection *The Song Celestial*, the translation of *Ghagavad Gita* (from The Mahabharata) by Sir Edwin Arnold. His poetic translation from Sanskrit text is so graceful as to be practically unrecognizable from the *Bhagavad-Gita* offered us by His Divine Grace, A.C. Bhaktivedanta Swami Probhupada, with its ongoing learned fundamentalist purports. The *Song Celestial* is as poetic as are David's *Psalms* or, as Dawkins so aptly observed, "the *Song of Songs*, and the sublime *Ecclesiastes*." And let us not forget the euphoria Jalaludin Rumi shares with us, his inspiration coming directly from the Koran. Any man whose translation fails to capture the spirit or the beauty of the scriptures misses the opportunity to raise the consciousness of the reader.

Bravo, Dr. Dawkins! As Burns and Wordsworth and Salinger would say, you're a Gentleman and a Scholar.

The original title of my book, as you might have guessed by scanning through the table of content, was to have been "*Pragmatic Realism*", but it sounded too much like a philosophical dissertation. Also, I don't have any delusions about being a philosopher, fewer still about following any particular religion, or betting my life on the latest scientific discoveries. I guess, we are just all people who believe in different things.

Yet, having taken some time to study both parties in the science/religion argument, it seems to me that they both carry equal force, and most certainly are equally as stubborn, equally as set in their ways, and most certainly equally as convinced that they are right. Nevertheless, the argument can never be settled, for the simple reason that one party argues from the intellectual and the other from the emotional point of view. I let you decide which is which, although don't be surprised if, at times, the demarcation line becomes blurry.

My learned 'inspirer' failed to mention what were the sources that, in turn, inspired both, the religions and the various sciences. Lao Tzu (the Old Master), Krishna, Buddha, Yeshûa, among others, men who did little more then try to alleviate the hardships of everyday life of their fellow men; who tried, through their own experience to show others how to be happy. And, by the way, not one of them ever claimed divinity. People who cannot live without an idol they can both, fear and adore, have imposed the title of god, or something akin to divinity, on them all. A strange predilection but, apparently extremely human, considering that those very masters did their best to dissuade their followers from doing just that. In a way, the great masters had all been Hedonists, determined to alleviate suffering from the human equation.

To alleviate suffering here and now.

It is indeed unfortunate that Mr. Dawkins spent so much time illustrating how people, masses of misguided people, managed to distort their teaching, rather than giving equal time to explaining the beauty of the original myths. I say myths, because it takes a great effort to try to uncover the truths, which the past masters attempted to impart to us.

In John 8:23, evidently growing desperate or at best frustrated, Yeshûa asks his disciples: "Why do ye not understand my speech?"

This sad, desperate cry is still ringing in my ears. Unfortunately the followers of religions were just as deaf as the scientists of the day. And, it seems, both remain deaf to this day.

Rather than enter into a preaching contest, I'll attempt to show that we, being a very, very primitive species, are extremely likely to be equally as wrong, whichever course we choose to guide our lives. The religionists choose essentially the emotional path, the scientists the intellectual. Perhaps that is what Einstein meant when he said as late as 1941 at the Symposium on Science, Philosophy *and* Religion, that *"Science without religion is lame, religion without science is blind."*

Atheists hate this quotation, assuming that because of it, Einstein was, or had been, misrepresented as a religious man. The problem they, the vast majority of the atheists, have is that of semantics. They have absolutely no idea what Einstein meant by the word religion, let alone by the concept of god. For the uninitiated, let me just say that the word 'religion' comes from Latin, meaning, 'to reconnect'. The question is, to what?

And there's the rub! The atheists don't know. Nor do most followers of various religions. Perhaps none of us know. Wasn't Einstein a genius? Alas, he's dead. He won't tell us. But for those who have no idea where to begin their search for the answer, try listening to Mozart's Requiem. It's a good start.

I'd suggest that we should not exclude an important part of the human nature while in the pursuit of knowledge. According to the old masters, we are fourfold-entities, integral in spiritual, mental, emotional and physical form. The first is responsible for ideas, the second for intellectual perambulations, the third for igniting those ideas with fire (to produce tangible results), and the final aspect that is little more than the consequence, or the result, which we may examine, carefully, to see how far we have strayed from the original idea.

We are life, and life is a learning process.

With regard to the intellect, I used the word perambulations with particular reference to science, in the original British meaning: to walk around (the parish, forest, or indeed, anywhere) in order to assert and record its boundaries. This is essentially what scientists do: they walk about, view, study as best they can, in order to record and assert boundaries of the object or idea they are examining. Unfortunately this approach is always limiting—it is setting boundaries. The better they define (the more dogmatic they become), the more they limit. This method, by itself, also removes the first trait of our make up, the 'spiritual' aspect. By that I mean that a scientist, by limiting himself to careful observation, precludes new ideas from infiltrating his dedicated purpose.

In spite of theoretical physicists' assurances that the act of observation changes the nature of that which is observed, the vast majority of scientists are satisfied with what's was there, though already isn't.

A sad 'observation' indeed.

Here again I chose to place inverted commas in the word 'spiritual', for the simple reason that I never met two people who agreed on the meaning of 'spirit'. The concept, however, is universal. Here's an excerpt from an essay I wrote in 1997 entitled *Spirit*. It is part of my *Beyond Religion II* collection. The essay is based, in part, on a book by Lyall Watson, the *Lightning Bird*.

> People living in northwestern Transvaal call themselves Ba Sotho. All things that are special to Ba Sotho have *moya*. The Polynesians call it *mana*. Both words have also been translated as wind, air, breath, spirit, soul and even life. In the Christian tradition, the Greek word *pneuma* has been translated as spirit, as had the Hebrew *ruach*, which also means wind and air. The Hebrews also have a word *neshamah*, which they translated variously as spirit or breath. Paul Twitchell, who wrote extensively on ancient religions, equates the words spirit and life as being synonymous, while defining the essence of soul as spirit. Thus between the Judeo-Christian tradition and some later writing attributing its knowledge to pre-Judaic scriptures, the Ba Sotho have covered all possible

meanings.

But only the Ba Sotho people give us an insight into the nature of spirit itself. According to Lyall Watson, Ba Sotho regard *moya* as "the essence of nature itself." Dr. Watson compares their vision of *moya* to electricity, as being powerful but as having no will or purpose of its own. They, the Ba Sotho, lay no claim as to its origin and suggest that, "it may simply exist." A few weeks ago a friend of mine came to see me. His eyes were shining with a new understanding. "There is no difference between spirit and matter," he said. He reached this conclusion in 86th year of his life. Were he and the Ba Sotho talking about the same thing?

In my reality, the words spirit, life, and consciousness, are synonymous. There is no life without consciousness; in both flora and fauna life manifests in different degrees, but life and consciousness remain synonymous. No ideas can touch our awareness when we are dead (not to be confused with 'spiritually' dead, which applies to people who knowingly shut off this gate of infinite knowledge.) As for physical 'death', I never met a person who was dead and conscious. I challenge any and all scientists to prove me otherwise. Of course, having walked about the parish, I do not equate physical cessation of biological functions with death. As I mentioned, our physical body is the result, not the cause of our being. In later chapters, we shall discuss what our body really is.

Don't hold your breath… it's not pretty.

My only way out was to try and leave out both: religions and science from this discussion. But as I could not make my points yet leave out both, emotions and intellect, completely from the equation (there would be no discernible result), I decided to resort to *Pragmatic Realism*. I'm sure that you'll find pages in this book where I appear to repeat the same maxims more than once. In my defense I can only plead that both scientists and religionists do so at least as often as I do, and, once again, I am unable to dismiss two aspects of my nature to sate your need for perfection. Ideas may be perfect, the resolutions seldom are. Contact me in a few million years. I'm sure I'll do better.

To make sure that we are on the same page, let us agree what we mean by Pragmatic Realism. There is absolutely no point in having a philosophy that does not support our view of reality. Thus if you wish to count yourself among people guided by a pragmatic approach, you can include in your philosophy only those assumptions that work satisfactorily, that are practical in the interpretation of reality as we understand it.

Also, the ideas must be testable.

There go the myths! Unless, of course, we can prove them, or at least some of them, as true. And the strangest thing of all is that if one eliminates the malignant growth, which religions have imposed on the original myths, more of them seem a great deal closer to the truth than originally (i.e. since the onset of the age of enlightenment began) imagined. In fact, science is only now beginning to find facts, which many a myth proposed millennia ago. One can but wonder what tomorrow might bring.

Yet here we encounter problems with our nature.

The problem with people is that, unbeknownst to them, they are continuously creating realities. The universe is an on-going process. Stars are born, and stars die. In this whirlwind of life, the religionists long to satisfy their emotional needs for stability, the scientists aim to satisfy their intellectual hunger for intellectual base, e.g.: the Higgs boson, sometimes referred to (yes, by scientists) as "the God particle". The priests, monks, preachers and their followers are in need of a god who will reward them for their good deeds, punish their enemies and, ultimately, grant them a way out—an eternal existence in heaven. Eternal boredom?

Scientists, on the other hand, are in need of a reality that makes, to them, some sort of logical sense. Einstein needed order and harmony and expected to find it in his equations. Now, even the velocity of light is being questioned. Both, religionists and scientists base their reality on transient phenomena. Their realities have both, a beginning and an end.

Pragmatic Realism needs neither. A pragmatic realist deals with events such as they are—not such as they want them to be. "I know... that I know nothing," said a wise man 2500 years ago. At long last, our ever-erring theoretical physicists have reached the state of embracing their ignorance—the premise that there are possibilities, at best probabilities, but no dogmas. If it weren't so, then the rest of eternity would be sheer hell for them.

Let us return to the roots of modern pragmatism.

The concept was (re)introduced in late nineteenth century by an American philosopher, logician, and mathematician, Charles Sander Peirce (1839—1914) about whom Bertram Russell, himself a philosophical heavyweight, wrote in 1959: "Beyond doubt (...) he was (...) certainly the greatest American thinker ever."

He, Peirce, postulated a maxim that an ideology or theory can only be true if—and only if—it works satisfactorily, and that the meaning of a proposition is to be found in the practical consequences of accepting it, and that impractical ideas are to be rejected. Here is the original 1878 statement:

> "It appears, then, that the rule of attaining the third grade of clearness of apprehension is as follows: Consider what effects, that might conceivably have practical bearings, we conceive the object of our conception to have. Then, our conception of these effects is the whole of our conception of the object."

Perhaps it should be noted that concepts of pragmatism are already present in the views of some ancient philosophers, including Xenophanes, Socrates, and Plato. Since this appears to be the place to reestablish our semantics, I wish to clarify what I mean by philosophy. Not the dictionary definition, but its origins. *Philos* (according to Wikipedia) "denoted a general type of love, used for love between family, between friends, a desire or enjoyment of an activity, as well as between lovers". *Sophia*, (or *Sofya*) quite simply meaning wisdom. And wisdom, to use the suggestion first offered by Emmet Fox, is a perfect blend of love and knowledge. The reconstruction of the word I leave to you.

***

PART ONE — THE PAST

"...all matter originates and exists only by virtue of a force which brings the particles of an atom to vibration which holds the atom together. We must assume behind this force is the existence of a conscious and intelligent mind. This mind is the matrix of all matter."

Max Planck 1858—1947
Novel Prize in Physics in 1918

Chapter 1
Fundamentalism in Religion and Science

*A fanatic is a man who consciously
over compensates
a secret doubt.*

Aldous Leonard Huxley,
British author (1894—1963)

Trying to argue for or against the existence of God leads to an unavoidable stalemate. The opposing parties have not agreed on the semantics, which would, or could, define the existence of the Infinite Source, yet both insist, as Albert Einstein had done, that Infinity exists. The physicist Max Plank (above) goes still further. He postulates, or at the very least suggests, the pre-existence of a mind which is a "matrix of all matter". As for infinity, Einstein, for his part, wasn't sure about the universe, but quite confident about his other candidate. No. The other candidate he was referring to was not the Infinite Source—it was human stupidity.

Although infinity cannot really be defined, we know the infinite by different names. As pointed out by Baruch Spinoza: "To define God is to deny God." Thus, the Infinite, or whatever moniker you wish to impose on God, cannot be defined without imposing limits on it. The word 'define' comes to us directly from Latin, *definire* meaning (inter alia) to limit, to explain, to bound as in set boundaries for, or to restrict. Not the sort of thing one would want to do with anything we like to think of as Infinite, particularly if we were to spell it with capital 'I'.

Furthermore, probability (of being right) dictated by the quantum theory should apply in equal measure to science and to myths. Though admittedly religions no longer qualify to be included in the divergent views of reality, one could say that Yeshûa was the Dawkins of his day, doing his best to free people from the mental and emotional oppression of the priests.

Perhaps, unfortunately, this is where the similarity ends. While Yeshûa confined himself to instilling faith in one's own potential, Dawkins tends to put the shackles of the ever-erring science on human consciousness. Why ever-erring? Because, we appear to change our minds every five minutes. Intellectually, we are, I am sorry to say, primitives.

Hence, I would suggest, we should preoccupy ourselves with little more than with Pragmatic Realism, as ancient myths appear to have done. As for (omnipresent?) intelligence, the Max Plank's mind, or an "infinite source"... they are another matter. We shall touch upon them throughout this book. The mind of an individual is, as we have seen in my little FOREWORD, quite another matter.

The only higher power Yeshûa, or Jesus as he was later known, recognized lay within himself. Charles Darwin (as does Dawkins with religious fervour) seems to externalize it by assigning it to the Universal Laws. Yeshûa, on the other hand, stated, quite clearly, that he and his 'father' (as he seemed to have referred to 'whatever was the absolute source of his power') are one.

Subjective experience is no less real and pragmatic than the so-called 'scientific' or objective experience that can be shared with, or by, others. All intangible experiences such as love, hate, a whole gamut of emotions, love or dislike of music, art... beauty in the eyes of the beholder... all that cannot be measured by human senses or by modern instrumentation, would have to be dismissed by an analytical/scientific mind. Yet we all must pass judgment on reality in which we find our being, whether we like it or not.

At least, in spite of popular belief, the followers of biblical teaching can be sure of one thing, though only if they actually *read* the Bible:

1. God does *not* pass judgment, ("...for the father (god) judges no man." John 5:22). Tell that to the millions of preachers and/or critics, who'd never read the Bible, or managed to diligently omit the items they found uncomfortable.

2. God *cannot* behold evil. ("You are of purer eyes than to behold evil, and cannot look on iniquity..." Habakkuk 1:13).

At least there is something that 'God' cannot do. Makes him almost... human, but contrary to us, the consequence of not being able to discern evil entails inability to pass judgment. On the other hand, the father "hath committed *all judgment* unto the *son*," (John 5:22). That's you and me. Yes, ladies are included. So far, so good. The Bible has set limits on the biblical Infinite but, so far, not on us.

"Ye are gods..." rings in my ears.

Anyone interested can find many confirmations of my selections throughout the Bible. Good luck.

Under the circumstances, at least for Jews and Christians, any discussion on the reality of good and evil as envisioned by believers, be they scientists or not, is entirely in our own hands. Or heads. Or whatever we use to be dogmatic and/or intolerant. We seem to find both traits quite easy to espouse. Buddhists already know what they are doing. They are just waiting to be awakened, while practicing the Eightfold Path. And the Four Noble Truths, of course, although I happen to disagree with one of them. I don't believe that "Life means Suffering". My book, *Key to Immortality* suggests why suffering is not necessary. Sorry Gautama, but, after all, the

Gospel of Thomas has been written some 600 years after you withdrew your consciousness from your physical body, and seekers of nirvana must have learned something new since.

A word about priesthood of yesteryear.

One cannot really blame the scientists for suffering from a good dose of fundamentalism. After all, for thousands of years, priesthood and scientists had been virtually synonymous. Only the priests had the means to study nature, not to mention the stars, and they alone declared their findings to people at large. Since our senses are extremely inefficient—we can see, for instance, but a minute, a really minuscule fragment of the wavelength of light surrounding us—the results of their scientific observations were not very reliable. It is to be hoped that scientists of today, having a more advanced technology and seemingly vast financial resources at their disposal, and being no longer constrained by dogmatic interferences from various churches and sacerdotal circles, will assure that the conclusions of their observations will be more trustworthy. Alas, not so. Many of the scientists continue to declare their finding dogmatically, continue to hate to be criticized, and then... change their mind.

Echoes of the past?

In early Judaism the priesthood was inherited through the families. While some Jews (e.g.: the Sadducees, who also fulfilled various political and religious roles including looking after the Temple, and the Karaites, meaning 'readers of the Hebrew scriptures'), claimed to have had their beliefs based on the written text, the Torah, most Jews appeared to have followed the Oral Law. The Pharisees (meaning 'set apart') took it upon themselves to transmit this Law to their remaining compatriots.

Yeshûa, as stated above, had little regard for the priesthood. He expressed his opinion about the priesthood quite clearly:

"But woe unto you, scribes and Pharisees, hypocrites! for ye shut up the kingdom of heaven against men: for ye neither go in yourselves, neither suffer ye them that are entering to go in." (Matthew 23:13)
Nothing changed.

Of course, Yeshûa (*Jesus*) taught that heaven is a state of consciousness, thus within us, an idea not picked up by the Christian religions to this day, and dismissed outright by scientists (with the exception of a few psychiatrists) as superstition.

"Why would anybody want to be happy here and now?" "Why would anybody want to find infinite potential within themselves?" they seem to ask. Yes, *they*, both of them, the priesthood and the scientists.

Perhaps that was why he, Yeshûa, had a number of other equally unpleasant and certainly undiplomatic things to say about the scribes and Pharisees. As I am sure, he would today about their counterparts.

Thus, the whole discussion about a resident or *in absentia* divinity is abortive. Still, both Dawkins and his opponents made a lot of chutzpa (and hopefully money), in their attempts to destroy each other. And I should mention, that I share most of the apostate author of *God Delusion* views regarding a whole gamut of religions, not, however, regarding reality. Also, religion has little, if anything, to do with 'god'. Look up the words of mystics on the subject and you'll agree, also. Words such as "Don't call me good, only my father is good and he's in heaven. Or... "Don't call me master," or... "The son of man can do nothing by himself." The scriptures demolish gods faster than I ever could. One day, we shall all agree. After all, are we not all latent Buddhas?

A word of caution. When referring to god as 'good father', we might bear in mind the words of Lao Tzu: "Tao is *impartial*—it always favours good men," (my italics).

In a dualistic reality, i.e. one based on the opposites of good and evil, only the state of balance is 'good'. There is a pragmatic saying that "God is what the opposites have in common". This is a great unwavering guideline for establishing the ethics of life. There is an old paradigm stating that there is no good without some evil, no evil without some good. If we ignore the 20-million deaths left in his wake, Hitler, from the point of view of eugenically inspired standards could claim to be 'good', or at least 'moral'. However, he was very far from the state of balance. Even as George W. Bush, evidently guided by the self-confessed and publicly announced new-born Christian status and with able, indeed eager, assistance of Toni Blair, is said (Opinion Research Business survey in Wikipedia) to have been at least in part responsible for the murder, or at least for the death, of approximately one million people. How is that for loving your enemy!

This is why I prefer to regard ethics as defining man's actions, while relegating morality to little more than keeping up with the Joneses and avoiding a public scandal.

Hence, Pragmatic Realism.

Without entering into the benefits or otherwise of various religions, a question arises how religious systems manage to survive longer that other systems designed to control man's minds. I am referring to social systems including all empires and political entities.

With regard to scientists, some evolutionary biologists have introduced *memes* as having properties necessary for evolution. (A little bit like the black matter in the universe, which is purported to help it collapse onto, or possibly into, itself). Essentially, a *meme* is an element of a culture or system which is, or can be, passed from one individual to another by non-genetic means, e.g. by imitation. It has been suggested that various religions, or cults, have survived, albeit for a very short time, due to memetic collaboration.

DELUSIONS

The proponents of this thesis may be right. I find it hard to imagine that genes (no matter how selfish) could, all by themselves, create monsters who would burn members of their own species on the stake.

Yet, as for longevity of some ecclesiastic organizations, I am inclined to disagree, especially as regarding religions that lasted longer than a century or two. In such cases, it is my contention that it is the threat of punishment and reward that keeps them going. Parents teach their children to be afraid at a very early age. In western religions, heaven and hell, the ultimate carrot and the ultimate stick, assure the religious system's survival. Throughout history, although less successfully, the same method had been attempted by various political entities. Genghis Khan, Hitler, Stalin, and only to a slightly lesser degree George W. Bush and his oligarchy, have all scared their people into abject submission. It is by far the easiest way to retain control over peoples' minds and modes of behaviour.

As for Buddhism, I never regarded it as religion. It is more what the western religions purport to be—a way of life.

The carrot and the stick have proven the most pragmatic method, even though it is completely divorced from reality. It does prove, however, that we, *en masse*, still expect to be treated like little children.

Interesting?

***

Chapter 2
Where We Were

Do what you can, with what you have, where you are.

Theodore Roosevelt, 26th U.S, President (1858—1919)

Not so long ago the Earth was flat. If you went sailing, and if you weren't careful, you might have slipped over the edge to your doom. Unless you were stopped by a 40-foot high wall of ice at the very edge of the earth/ocean, which would also smash your boat to pieces—a dubious choice of impending demise. The modern hypotheses of the Flat Earth Society created not so long ago by Samuel Rowbotham (1816–1884), is still doing quite well in the USA. Though originating in the UK, its 'modern' version, founded by another Englishman, Samual Shenton in 1956, was later led by Charles K. Johnson, who made his home in Lancaster, California. The Society was inactive after the American's death in 2001, but was quickly resurrected by its new president, Daniel Shenton, in 2004.

The late president, Charles Johnson, thus expressed the aims of the Society:

> "To carefully observe, think freely, rediscover forgotten fact and oppose theoretical dogmatic assumptions. ...To replace the science religion... with SANITY."

Surely, all noble sentiments. A little of what I am attempting to do, right now. We all try to do this, at least those of us who have not yet been dragged into the quagmire of fundamentalism of science or religion. As Einstein said, "Education is what remains after one has forgotten everything he learned in school." He was referring to other peoples' knowledge. Not knowledge coming from within. A number of poets, musicians, scientists, and mystics admitted to having woken up, after a good night's sleep, with new, sometimes revolutionary, ideas. Subconscious at work? Perhaps. But, what of the unconscious?

There are other things that a well-trained scientific mind must dismiss as irrelevant, or at least *non sequitur*. There is a story about Einstein (who was said to have been a very stupid child) that he has only shed his presumed obtuseness after his mother bought him a violin. Even after leaving school, Einstein played Mozart or Bach to help him with his equations. Not a very scientific approach but, at least for me, Einstein was first a philosopher, and only then a scientist. In the old days, philosophers have had to be mathematicians. I suppose 'physicist' is the next best thing. By that I mean that his scientific theories were the result of his philosophy and logic, not the other way round. He is said to have even used the fiddle to improve on his equations. No mention of genes or memes.

So much for scientific method.

Of course, in spite of the Flat Earth Society, our scientists have made enormous strides since 2004. Most of them accept that the Earth is fairly round. I am told that since condemning Galileo Galilei (1564—1642), and burning Giordano Bruno (1548—1600) at the stake as heretic for sharing Copernican (Miłołaj Kopernik 1473—1543) views, even the Vatican accepted the notion.

For now. Until the next revelation?

We must never forget that the Vatican Observatory (Papal interest in astronomy dates back to 1578) is a scientific research institute of the Holy See subject to the Governorate of Vatican City State. Rather like Royal Astronomical Society (founded in 1820), or the American Astronomical Society (est. in 1899), only... much, much older. In fact the Vatican Observatory is one of the oldest astronomical institutes on earth.

Perhaps old and good are not synonymous in science, although the astronomers continue to study starlight of stars long dead.

As for revelations, past or future, I suggested in my book, *Visualization—Creating Your Own Universe,* that all visions are subjective.

"Subjective religious visions are called Revelations. Subjective non-religious visions (unless held by famous people) are often referred to as hallucinations. Hallucinations can be subdivided into artistic, political, social, idealistic, and a whole array of inspired non-religious fantasies, delusions or insights. Revelations fall essentially into two categories, the pragmatic (aimed at organizing people) and the prophetic (aimed at scaring people). Both deal with influencing others directly. There has never been a prophecy of a carrot that was not accompanied by a stick. The prophetic visions are usually symbolic in nature, i.e. misunderstood by all people who attempt to give them a fundamentalist interpretation. There is a very basic characteristic of all visions. They can never really be shared. People who claim allegiance to a vision of another human being become followers, never those who implement the original vision."

Nevertheless, as you can see, good ideas seldom die, and if their originators do, there are always others who seem more than willing to pick up the banner, and joyfully make fools of themselves. I should know. I used to be quite dogmatic myself. I once held dogmatic faith in both, science and religion.

Yet, in spite of the Flat Earth Society's persistent efforts,

DELUSIONS

the scientists decided to forsake sanity and to round off the edges of Earth into an irregular globe. For their sake I have placed this whole chapter in THE PAST.
I shall return to this matter in THE PRESENT.

Alas, you can't win them all.

In the meantime, other scientists (particularly the astrophysicists but other specialties obediently followed suit) decided that it all started, and I mean ALL, with the Big Bang. No one cared to define just how big the bang was, but who cares about details. Scientists deal mostly with things so small that they cannot see them or, although very large, so far away that they cannot see them. A harmonious equilibrium? And after all, at the time of the big bang there was only one universe to worry about. Today, they would probably say 'a' rather then 'the' big bang.

Nevertheless, even with just one universe, this new cosmological model calls for a really enormous Big Bang, some 13.7 billion years ago. Ever since then the Universe continued to expand, on and on, and would continue to do so until it runs out, they said, of the original momentum, at which time it would slow down to a momentary standstill, and then would begin to collapse to its original form. Actually, originally the universe had no form, there was, apparently nothing before the Big Bang, but, as we all know, what goes up, must come down. Ergo—the Big Crunch was proposed.

Unfortunately there was a problem. There was not enough mass (matter to laics) to create sufficient gravitational pull to make the universe contract upon itself.

No problem, said the theoretical cosmologists.

Since there is no God to do the work for us (as the believers believe He did at the very beginning, before the scientists thought of the Big Bang), let us suppose, they said, (the scientists, not the believers) that there is matter that we cannot see, or measure, or smell, or... detect with our state-of-the-art instruments. Let us give it a scientific name, they said, and call it Dark Matter, which, now that it's named, will provide the necessary reverse impetus. Oh, yes. And if there isn't enough Dark Matter, we'll think of something else. Like Dark Energy, for instance. Not just so dark as to be invisible to our eyes, but outside the ultra violet and/or infrared spectrum. A sort of Dark Light.

Good idea! After all, Einstein did say that imagination was more important than knowledge, and the scientists were very short of the latter commodity.

In 1934 Fritz Zwicky postulated the existence of Dark Matter (not to be confused with Antimatter, Dark energy, Dark fluid, Dark flow or anything visible at all—a little like God, although God, according to believers, could also be light yet remain invisible). This would account for the missing mass in the orbital velocities of galaxies and suchlike. In no time at all, the invisible Dark Matter was observed (sic!) in rotational speeds of galaxies in clusters. Later, it was confirmed in the temperature distribution of hot gas in galaxies and clusters of galaxies.

Bingo!

Oops!

The Universe continued to expand!

No problem, said the learned scientists. We've already thought of Dark Energy. Let us postulate that it is an invisible energy, which pushes the universe on its wild ride into the unknown. In the standard model of cosmology (that's scientific lingo to describe what we thought of last), Dark Energy currently accounts for 73% of the total mass-energy of the universe.

With a little effort, we shall make the whole universe invisible, and ask God to create a new one.

***

Chapter 3
What We Were

The results of political changes are hardly ever those which their friends hope or their foes fear.

Thomas Huxley, British biologist (1825—18950)

Forget invisible matter and equally invisible energy and listen to us, said the priesthood. Our ideas are much better. If we read exactly what is written in the Bible, some 6000 years ago, the Almighty God had created us. At least Adam was created. Eve was built-up around one of our ribs. No disrespect intended, but, if we are to believe the fundamentalists, it was the best the Almighty could do. At least we (men, or one of us) weren't lonely anymore.

Then we screwed up. Adam and Eve did. They ate an apple from the tree of knowledge and got kicked out from Eden. Seems like a harsh punishment for eating a lousy apple. On the other hand, maybe Eden wasn't all that much after all.

Anyway, we went forth and began to multiply, and multiply, and multiply, and didn't stop to this day. In fact, we continue to multiply. We're about to hit 7 billion! Maybe we did, already. Who can tell in this crowd? I bet neither Adam nor Eve would have ever guessed it. Had they known, they probably would have left that apple alone. Boy, did we ever multiply?

That's the popular version.

Earlier, some 3 million years earlier, before anyone thought of an Almighty God, some apes developed a forward propelling toe, which enabled them to walk forward on a flat terrain with much greater dexterity. Encouraged by their toe, they soon came down from trees, and got down (no pun intended) to the business of leading a life on earth. This bunch of primates had a long way to go.

We had been given all sorts of funny names. Depending where or when our bones were found, and possibly for some other reasons, they were given different names. The oldest were, reputedly, *Australopithecus afarensis*. A little later, paleontologists came up with another unpronounceable name, the *Ardipithicus ramidus*, whose bones were said to reach back some five million years.

Some people think a lot of their bones.

I heard of a construction site where work has been delayed for six months because during excavation the contractor had found some supposedly human bones, which instantly became sacred to the First Nations. To this day I have no idea how they knew they were sacred. The delay cost the developer a small fortune.

Finally, after at least ten different species, at long last came *Homo sapiens,* followed by *Homo sapiens sapiens*. That's us. We, the Hss, have been around for some 200,000 years. *Homo sapiens*, the species to which we all belonged until very recently, is now regarded as the link between *Homo erectus* and *Homo sapiens sapiens*. The *Homo neanderthalensis* got lost somewhere in the translation. He is now regarded as a completely different species. No matter. Or maybe not. We shall see...

So much for old bones.

Later, much later, we have been told that at the time of conception, a soul, an external entity, invaded us, or our bodies, and stayed with us until we died—or until we were excommunicated, in which case we suffered eternal damnation at a place called hell. Those who were not excommunicated, providing they were non-atheists, were still free to go to heaven, after they died of course, unless they were really nasty, in which case, after their bodies were buried, their souls went on to purgatory. After they got cleaned up, they would rise to heaven, where they remained, presumably bored stiff, for ever-after. And that's a very long time to be bored.

If we decided to be atheists, we could do anything we wanted to do, because we didn't have to have a soul. Nor did a soul have to have us. We were free.

By the way, the Christian hell is reserved exclusively for Christians, with the membership later extended to include the Moslem, and is not to be confused with Sheol, Gehenna, Hades, the Valley of Hinnom, Tartarus, or a number of other resorts that are not nearly as nasty as the Christian/Moslem God/Allah has determined for his exclusive members. On the other hand, it is a well known fact, that many people are well capable of creating private hells for themselves right here, on Earth, but such are usually terminated on their departure from their bodies, referred to as dying. Later, after they die, they are free to start again. That is known as reincarnation. Of course for that, you need a soul. No soul—no incarnation. Sorry. Unless you have an Atma, of course.

But it would be grossly unfair to call your attention to hell, without giving equal time to heaven. Sometime ago, I had occasion to write an essay entitled *Heaven*. At the risk of offending some people, here are some excerpts (with small adaptations).

"Some very religious followers think that if they blow themselves to kingdom come while murdering some innocent people who disagree with their demands, they will take the elevator directly to paradise where they will be instantly surrounded by forty beautiful concubines, or women, or wives. (I am told this has been upgraded to 72 virgins). I have a slight problem with this image of the ever-after, but that's probably because I enjoy, right now, quite enough problems with just one, single concubine, aah... woman, aah... wife. Actually she is whatever she chooses to be. I recall Shakespeare's prognosis: I *know I am too mean to be your queen, and yet too good to be your concubine.* Perhaps in heaven she can be all three. I'll just do my best to enjoy them all.

Then there are those who'd rather recline on puffed-up, fluffy clouds, surrounded by ever-smiling, perhaps also seventy-two, angels strumming their golden harps. I strongly suspect the angels would be attired in Mozartesque regalia, and be conducted by the immaculately tailed, fiddling Tarzan, known to the aficionados as André Rieu. They would play on and on and on. Forever and ever..."

"And then we have the serious guys (and dolls).

They (we) will spend their (our) eternity at the feet of their (our) chosen deity (catalogue available at the gate), basking in His (Her) glory, rejoicing with the (above mentioned) angels. They (we) will be peeking down, way down, (with just the most innocuous of smirks) at the poor saps who still didn't even make it to the antechamber of the heavenly palace. Here we shall luxuriate in lavish and eternal peace, serenity, and peace. And serenity. Our joy will in no way be tempered by our knowledge (we shall be fairly omniscient) that our aunt and uncle, possibly also that second cousin (she was a bitch), are frying dead (though seemingly alive) on the sharp prongs of the glowing spits wielded by the long-tailed and horned (if not horny) devils.

Anyone for Florida?"

"Surely for the godfearing awaits a place of security, gardens and vineyards and maidens with swelling breasts, like of age, and a cup overflowing."

This is another option offered by the Qu'ran in Sura

LXXVIII, *The Tiding.*
To each his (her?) own.

Does any of this have anything to do with the Bible? Well, if we take the symbolic meaning, the story changes, well... fundamentally.
"So God created man in his own image, in his own image created he him." (Genesis 1:27)
or... (see Chapter 13, then come back).
"So the undefined objects of worship, (presumably some sorts of states of universal consciousness), created Adam in their image, making him, likewise, an individualized state of consciousness"
And nothing more.
How do we know? Because only in chapter 3 verse 21 of Genesis, "unto Adam and his wife did Lord God (*Elohim*, i.e.: objects of worship) made coats of skin, and clothed them." Just think about it. They not only were naked but *they had no skins!* Obviously God didn't sew actual coats, as in fur-coats, for the couple. Since a moment ago, and probably for a few billion years—there is no time in Paradise, remember, it's like heaven—they were stark naked (in fact bodiless), had they put on real fur-coats they would have burned up with heat. And think of the smell...
Now that was long after Eve had given Adam the apple (Women! You can't live with them, and according to the Objects of Worship, you can't live without them). Surprising though it may seem, the apple came from the 'tree' of knowledge, making Adam aware that he was no longer just a free, individualized state of consciousness able to spend eons gallivanting around Eden, not even worried about any physical skin, let alone a body. But worst of all, Adam became aware of his ego, the single most powerful trait of alienation. He no longer felt an integral, inseparable part of the omnipresent consciousness. He felt apart. Kicked out. He became aware of duality.

How do I know? Because there is no time without duality. Time is a function of the physical universe, not one consisting exclusively of a state of consciousness wherein whatever you imagine—is. Do you remember how much you could do in a single dream?

The holiday was over. Adam became aware of duality, and he became part of it. He had a body. He also became aware of good and evil (Genesis 3:22). Before that, he was like god, he couldn't behold evil. His eyes were too pure. And now? And now he'd spend the rest of his existence trying to find his way back. It will take a long time. Aren't we all still trying?

Alas, his devolution had begun.

At least, that what the Bible says. Not the nonsense you hear from the fundamentalists. While, as I have already pointed out, the Bible is written in a highly symbolic idiom, making it virtually incomprehensible to fundamentalists, scientific and religious alike. Even when deciphered, though it then reads like guidelines for the living (or how to be happy regardless of circumstances), the reader is not to regard himself as a product of biological evolution (sorry Charles), but as a spiritual being using the biological construct as a means to experience the process of becoming.

The biologists and their scientifically minded confreres who do not study symbolism, nor do they venture into the mystical nature of man, will, as far as the Bible is concerned, remain for now in the dark.

To cheer up the late developers who say that since vast majority of people take the Bible literally they can't all be wrong, let me suggest an equal number does not understand quantum mechanics, yet not one of the stubborn scientific fundamentalists claims that therefore the quantum theory must be wrong. Furthermore, a number of biblical stories have been known long before biblical times, yet, in spite of the extended Kindergarten, they continue to be taken literally, rather than as stories designed to illustrate *spiritual* truth. It seems that indeed, many are called but few are chosen. The vast majority of people choose the easy way out, a way not requiring any effort or study, or hours of contemplation; they *choose* to remain ignorant.

When fully understood, the Bible is a superb handbook of Pragmatic Realism.

The doubters should not be that surprised when we consider that among the countless millions, now billions, of people, there are indeed very few to match Mozart, or Beethoven, or Verdi, or Shakespeare, or Yeshûa, or Buddha, or any giants of the human species, exceptional or chosen people, who left those millions and billions behind. And even then, the vast majority of people prefer to listen to American Idol than to Georgian Chant or an operatic aria. The ultimate consolation is that our true self is immortal, time a figment of our imagination, and ultimately we are all latent, dormant, if slightly retarded Buddhas. Our time will come.

***

Richard P. Feynman (1918 - 1988)
Albert Einstein Award (1954)
E. O. Lawrence Award (1962)
Nobel Prize in Physics (1965)
Oersted Medal (1972)
National Medal of Science (1979)

Some quotes...

"It doesn't seem to me that this fantastically marvelous universe, this tremendous range of time and space and different kinds of animals, and all the different planets, and all these atoms with all their motions, and so on, all this complicated thing can merely be a stage so that God can watch human beings struggle for good and evil - which is the view that religion has. The stage is too big for the drama."

"Religion is a culture of faith; science is a culture of doubt."

"Science is like sex: sometimes something useful comes out, but that is not the reason we are doing it. "

"If you thought that science was certain - well, that is just an error on your part."

"The highest forms of understanding we can achieve are laughter and human compassion."

Chapter 4
The God Diffusion

A bad book is as much of a labor to write as a good one, it comes as sincerely from the author's soul.

Aldous Leonard Huxley, British author (1894—1963)

Perhaps this is the right place to express my gratitude to Richard Dawkins. His many books had provided me with many hours of pleasure. And now, his *God Delusion* inspired me to offer *not* an opposing view, but, hopefully, a complementary one to his stringent defense of human mind, *vis à vis* human emotions, imagination, let alone spirit. Thus my book, *Delusions*, subtitled *Pragmatic Realism*, does not deny Mr. Dawkins's dislike for religions, but broadens the sphere of mind controlling philosophies. As for my quotation above, that of the British author Huxley, the problems start when the author denies having one. If he denies having soul—at least that's Aldous Huxley's opinion.

I might add, that there are many other areas where Dr. Dawkins and I agree. I wholly support his views on the inherent 'evils' of absolutism; on his decrying of tolerance towards others. Also I fully understand and share his scathing condemnation of American, not to mention British, Pakistani, or Afghan self-righteous bigotry. I find it particularly repulsive in "the land of the free", where the Star-spangled Banner is indeed spangled with moral and physical blood of many who are not free at all.

Regrettably, the many are, and will most likely remain, "the masses." They represent the vast majority who have forsaken spiritual (*not* religious but spiritual) development, and have concentrated on amassing the benefits of "natural selection". Perhaps now, through his own arguments, the good doctor will believe, or at least examine, the eastern concept of devolution. It seems valid from Pragmatic Realism point of view.

This chapter deals with, no, not 'Delusion', which Dawkins so aptly argued, but Diffusion, as in dissemination, transmission, flow, dispersion or, quite simply, omnipresence. Not faith in a polytheistic god, but the omnipresence of intelligence, life and other attributes of the universe, which instigate and sustain evolution.

As in Universal Laws.

In fact, though our renowned atheist might vehemently deny it, he simply substituted the word Laws, for God, which, he evidently believes qualifies him to call himself an atheist. Yet it is evident that he, as well as his hero, not to say idol, Charles Darwin, both appear to recognize the word 'Laws' as an adequate substitute for the force motivating the universe and all that's in it, to act in a reasonably rational, ever-improving, progressive way.

What's in a name?

In the sense of dismissing a 'religious' concept of god, I most certainly am an atheist, too, although I'd prefer to assign some name to that force that would include benevolence, intelligence and, perhaps even compassion without judgment. Not an easy trio of traits to fulfill. Why benevolence? Because I firmly believe that without such the universe would have long disappeared, either in the vastness of absolute zero, or in an all-annihilating big crunch (which astrophysicists love so much). I leave it to the scientists to choose their preferred option. By the way, the absolute zero is a hell that our sacerdotal friends haven't thought of. As yet.

Yes. I truly believe that we, humans, are in great need of infinite compassion. We seem to have inexhaustible ability to act in most stupid, contemptible way imaginable towards each other, contrary to any logic, common sense or scientific dictates. Just imagine, after some 3 billion years of 'evolution' (or even 6000 years, as reckoned by Christian/Jewish religious fundamentalists), the last century is recognized by many as the bloodiest, the most murderous, in the history of man.

Is this what is meant by evolution? Our enhanced ability and willingness to kill each other?

The total number of deaths during the World War 2 has been calculated at between 50 and 70 million. The best known and by far the most often repeated figures are those of some 6,000,000 Jews having died in the Holocaust. According to the Jewish Virtual Library of the Simon Wiesenthal Centre, the Holocaust account for 5,860,000 deaths, which the Library rounds off to 6,000,000.

That leaves some 54,000,000 non-Jews, who are seldom mentioned. But even those figures pale in comparison to total number of deaths during the 20th century. According to Piero Scaruffi (URL provided below), 160 million people died in a variety of wars during the 20th century. Further references are provided for your personal research.

> http://www.scaruffi.com/politics/massacre.html
> http://necrometrics.com/20c5m.htm
> http://necrometrics.com/pre1700a.htm#20worst

Other statisticians cheer us on with the thought that in the present millennium we are likely to break all previous records. Of course, there are more of us to kill. Since 1999, we are in danger of adding a cool billion 'live' people before the end of 2011. We are encouraged in this endeavour by all religions and other tax-collecting organizations. They are both encouraging the masses to increase their number, to go forth and multiply, in order to increase the numbers on their collection plates, and of their tax base. After all, someone has to pay for those who produce nothing, right? And don't forget their pensions. Perhaps Einstein was right about the only infinity we could really be sure of.

I'd suggest that science, or scientists, who through the invention of masses of mass-destruction weapons greatly contributed to the efficacy with which one human can kill another, contributed in some measure to this progress. Or is it to evolution? Perhaps, in their wisdom, they were just trying to keep down the population explosion. If so, then they failed. Is this what Natural Selection led us to?

Dawkins states: "Natural Selection (is): the process which, as far as we know, is the only process ultimately capable of generating complexity out of simplicity."

I beg to differ. Well, sir, perhaps you ought to have a chat with my wife regarding the menu, when we expect friends for dinner; or listen to any politician delivering his address on economy; or anyone trying to explain poetry.

Seriously, though, let us try the human mind. Not brain—mind. Simple ideas seem to originate in simple minds—like one belonging to the son of a carpenter—and grow, without the aid of natural selection, to sweep the world. Ideas like *love your neighbour*. Or *do unto others as you'd have them do unto you.* Are these simple ideas or complex ones. How come so few people can understand them?

Or one might try listening to some Mozart piano progressions. Or Bach's counterpoint. Or it would not hurt anyone to read *"Complexity—The Emerging science at the edge of Order and Chaos"* by M. Mitchell Waldrop. A most excellent book. Of course, most people I know are concerned more with the evolution of human thought than with a bug becoming buggier. Or aren't humans allowed to evolve any more? Perhaps the biologists have joined the ranks of the followers of Esoteric Buddhism. However, *chacun à son goût*. Frankly, if evolution is to explain to us the nature of things, I'd rather side with Lucretius, (Titus Lucretius Carus, ca. 99BCE—ca. 55BCE), a Roman poet and philosopher. His epic poem *"De rerum natura,"* (*On the Nature of Things*), appeals to the inherent Epicureanism in my Hedonistic nature. And let us never forget that Lucretius followed in the footsteps of Democritus, who seemed to admire empty space as much as the nearly 'empty' atoms thinly dispersed within it. And you'll soon learn (in Chapter 7) how I feel about empty space.

While I share profound distaste for all the sacerdotal classes which under the guise of religious precepts attempt, all too often successfully, to dictate and impose their beliefs on others, I cannot, in good faith, dismiss some, albeit few and far between exceptions, such as St. Francis of Assisi, Father Pio and a number of mystics, as having any ambition in mind other then to serve humanity by their own example. They, those few, didn't *tell* others what to do—they *showed* them. And until I shall find an equal number of atheists who do likewise, I shall reserve my judgment as to the superiority of philosophy espoused by the opposing parties.

Having said that, we have the glaring problem of a number of people who have been nominated as the originators of myths, which later became distorted into religious beliefs. Contrary to the advocates of atheism (in the religious sense myself among them), I share the ancient adage attributed to Socrates, that "unexamined life is not a life worth living". If there are atheists who espouse this sentiment, I am not aware of them. To do so one would have to define life as more than a biological entity. For the most part, the few I've met seem much too busy fighting that which they don't believe in. Which that which they don't believe exists. They seem inspired by Don Quichotte.

But we must be careful.

Krishnamurti warns us that, "Self-knowledge is not knowing oneself, but knowing every movement of thought... So watch every movement of thought, never letting one thought go without realizing what it is. Try it. Do it and you will see what takes place."

Nevertheless, to paraphrase Socrates, until atheists' lives are examined, I shall refrain from assigning my opinion. Since I am essentially a Hedonist, (my only restriction being that I do not, knowingly, derive my pleasure at someone else's expense), and I freely admit that scientists have contributed somewhat (oh, all right, a great deal) to my everyday comfort, I am still more impressed with the man who said, "These things have I spoken unto you, that my joy might remain in you, and that your joy might be full." He taught us how to live.

Now we come to the real problem that might appear to contradict a lot of what I said in my preceding paragraphs. While it is true that Paul of Tarsus should be accorded the authorship of the Christian religions, the same cannot be said of Yeshûa, (or Yehoshûa—meaning Jah is salvation), who became known in the West, under the Greek influence, as Jesus.

As for Paul, there is a quandary. If the Vatican crowded with highly educated clergy are to this day completely incapable, as are their secular Ph.D. counterparts from Oxford, Cambridge, Yale, Harvard, or Sorbonne, of understanding the teaching of Christ, then how can we blame Paul or Tarsus, an ex-Pharisee, whom Yeshûa called, false teachers, hypocrites and offspring of vipers, whose pre-conversion activities included the persecution of Christ's followers, for getting it wrong?

Since the publication of the documents known as The Nag Hammadi Library, we, "the ordinary people", no longer have that excuse. Unless we are afraid to read it under the possible threat of anathema. As one of those commoners, I had occasion to offer my commentary on one of the ancient manuscripts, *The Gospel of Thomas.*

As for myself, having been brought up as a Roman Catholic, later educated by Jesuits, I have not come across anyone who ever knew, or shared their knowledge with me, as to the meaning of the name Jesus. We are, nevertheless, given some hints regarding his nature in the scriptures.

Here are some quotations from the King James Bible, attributed to Yeshûa.

"Why do you call me good? None is good, except one, that is, God." (Luke 18:19) Perhaps we may have to revise our concept of what we mean by 'good'?

"Kingdom of God is within you," (Luke 17:21). This statement defines heaven as a state of consciousness. Also, Kingdom of God is usually referred to as heaven. Thus heaven is within us and, therefore... so is God.

"I am not your master..." (Gospel of Thomas, logion 13). Speaking to Thomas, his disciple.

"My father which is in heaven" (Matthew 12:50) and... "Heaven is within you." As previously quoted from the Gospel of Thomas. Please note, not just within 'me', but also YOU. Yeshûa was not just speaking about himself but about all of us.

And the Gospel of Thomas further assures us that "heaven is within you and without you". I might add, 'here and now'.

To confuse the matter thoroughly, once and for all:
Heaven is within us.
God is in heaven.
Therefore God is within us.
Or, if you prefer:
God is omnipresent, therefore God is within us, and likewise, therefore we are within God.

This may revise, somewhat, our concept of what is God,

but I hope the above makes it reasonably clear what the scriptures have to say about it. If one is a Christian, that's all one has to believe in. The rest will become easy. Or, you can ignore the Bible and do your own thing. We have freewill, remember? Or... do we?

Thus no one in his or her wildest dreams could possibly accuse Jesus Christ of presenting himself as God. Son of God—yes, not God the son. He hastens to explain that, "*all* who do the will of the father are children of the most high," (my italics). In fact the statement stating that, "ye are gods," dates back to King David's 82nd psalm. If we are to believe the fundamentalists' chronological calculations, King David lived between 1037BC and 967BC, thus most psalms must have been written about that time, (although some of them may have been written by others, around 539BC, after Jewish exile in Babylon). Either way, both authors/composers date back to long before Yeshûa was born. By no stretch of imagination can we blame Yeshûa for making up stories about our own aspirations to his or anyone else's divinity. The idea had been long established, and just as long ignored, by the Jewish/Christian tradition.

Not very pragmatic, but very real.

Thus, you and I, providing we obey the laws, presumably those referred to by Charles Darwin, are the sons and daughters of the same progenitor, or as I prefer to think of it, of the Creative (evolutionary) Force of the Universe, (referred to by Darwin as Laws). Of course, I'd suggest that all these statements refer to our states of consciousness, not our overfed, abused and/or misused physical bodies. Even the most avid atheists no longer think of God as an androgynous anthropomorphic super-animal 'created', before the Big Bang, unto the image and likeness of man.

But the problem lies deeper. Like most scientists, religionists invariably tend towards fundamentalism. As they are more or less compelled take the scientific treatises literally, and they are inclined to do likewise with the Bible. The man who inspired this book is no exception. And there lies the fundamental (no pun intended) problem. The Bible deals almost exclusively with our state (s) of consciousness. If taken literally it is indeed a document that doesn't make much sense. To use Dawkins's literary interpretation:

"The God of the Old Testament is arguably the most unpleasant character in all fiction: jealous and proud of it; petty, unjust, unforgiving control-freak; vindictive, bloodthirsty ethnic cleanser; a misogynistic, homophobic, racist, infanticidal, genocidal, filicidal, pestilential, megalomaniacal, sadomasochistic, capriciously malevolent bully."

I might mention that the Bible is only fiction to the degree to which all the philosophical and/or psychological dissertations that use 'stories' to illustrate their theses, are fiction. I might repeat that, in the Bible, any resemblance to historical facts, if any, is purely coincidental.

Indeed, to believe in such a God as described, by my learned hero, in such a fundamentalist manner, one would have to apply and espouse all the adjectives to oneself. After all, aren't we created unto His image and likeness? If, however, anyone were to spend an hour or two (perhaps a little longer...) studying my *"Dictionary of Biblical Symbolism,"* none of the above would apply. Perhaps scientists are not disposed towards symbolism.

Even a cursory study of the documents of the Nag Hammadi Library would further disband the nonsense perpetrated by the fundamentalists. Here, too, I might refer the reader to my *Key to Immortality*, which attempts to unravel the wisdom of the Gospel of Thomas. While Bishop Irenaeus (2nd century AD) of Lugdunom (now Lion in France) who had been canonized most probably for his infamous *"Adversus Haereses",* or *Against Heresies*, might be forgiven for attempting to destroy Gnosticism, which I would describe as the subjective equivalent of scientific method of objective observation of the past or dead matter (see later chapters). The critics of today have no such excuse. Irenaeus was fighting for his church. All too often the atheists of today seem to be fighting for their ego, thus displaying equal narrowness of mind. Rather as Irenaeus had. Some later saints, I might add 'of dubious sanctity', were no exceptions, as were later scientists.

***

Chapter 5
The Beginning and the End

*Pragmatism asks its usual question.
"Grant an idea or belief to be true," it says, "what concrete difference will its being true make in anyone's actual life? How will the truth be realized? What experiences will be different from those which would obtain if the belief were false?"*

William James
American psychologist and philosopher (1842—1910)

Infinity has neither beginning nor end. If it had, it would not be infinite. We would live in the past, or future, but not in the present. Not in the NOW. Yet... as William Blake would say in his *Auguries of Innocence*, would we, (you and I) but, "Hold infinity in the palm of your hand, And eternity in an hour."

Ah, yes. Poetry is not an exact science...

We tend to confuse the tangible with the intangible, the visible with the invisible, the manifested with that which is not manifested—as yet. There is a reason for it.

Frankly, we've got it all wrong. We, or at least all the scientists I've ever met, live in the past. We, or they, ignore the present. The NOW. The true reality.

We study the light of distant stars that, all too often, is already dead—only the light, the information about them, reaches us with delays of, sometimes, millions of years. Yes, many of those stars are very, very dead. We do the same with the galaxies; we try to reach, backwards, to the first nanoseconds after the 'big bang' that might have never really taken place. We only think it had. If it had ever taken place, it also died somewhere, in the antiquity of billions of years. And, after all, a big bang would have to be followed by a big crunch. Alas, as already discussed in Chapter 2: *Where We Were*, there is not enough mass in the universe to pull us together again; to reverse the 'ever-expanding' universe. No matter. When we cannot find observations to fit our theories then we invent items like dark matter, or dark energy, to fit our inept concepts of reality. We employ the same method when studying our bodies, our physical bodies, pretending that we are studying reality, and not the shadow that reality has left behind. Alas, even that doesn't work. Of late, the theoretical scientists had spent billions of our hard earned dollars to 'prove' that the universe not only isn't about to shrink, but that it continues to expand ever-faster. And how do they know this? By studying the past. The long, long dead past. They study light, photons, that left the stars thousands of years ago. To repeat, stars that might well be dead. They study the corpses. Like our physicians. The cells in our bodies are in a continuous process of renewal. All the cells. And what to the physicians study? The cells that are dying, or are already dead. They are studying those left behind.

Yes, we definitely live in the past. This may prove to be a recurrent theme in this book. I often think that we have forgotten more than we shall ever learn. Distant echoes of Golden Age?

So let us look at our past. No, not biblical, or even scientific. Let us look at our lore. Once I wrote yet another essay. I called it *Vanishing Worlds*. You may find it amusing. It is in Volume I of my *Beyond Religion* collections. I made a few changes to make it belong in this book. Here's part of it.

"I had a vision.

In it, each man and woman was a universe interconnected with every other man and woman by that which they each held in common. That shared, or objective, universe was but a tiny fraction of the richness of ideas, thoughts, dreams, hopes, which fomented within their individual minds. But it was objective. It was that which was common to most of them. It was that which they agreed on. It was a point of reference. That's all. Just a point of reference.

A critical mass of shared ideas determines the nature of the universe detectable to our physical senses.

In the past, such old, now dissolved worlds, had been handed down to us as lore: Mu, Lemuria, Atlantis, had all been very real to the men and women who inhabited those conglomerates of ideas, we call an objective universe. As we progress, evolve, the subjective mind rejects the old to make room for the new. Most people find it difficult to accept that Lemuria or Atlantis ever existed.

Well, they did, but not in the way we imagine.

Could our glorious universe cease to exist, as did the worlds of our past? The stars, galaxies... trees, flowers, mountains and oceans... the human heritage of culture, civilizations? Was the earth once flat? Could a sailor fall over the edge—if he believed in it hard enough? Does an adamant, unshakeable faith have the power to create reality? Or is it always the same, tired, polluted, exploited, eternal universe—in which only we are changing....

No, surely this could never be."

Generations of men speculated on the immortality of soul. Later, when our consciousness became more material, we speculated mostly on possibilities of prolongation of physical life, of our material bodies. From that moment on, we began looking for Ambrosia—for the nectar of immortality. We haven't stopped to this day. Why?

In my vision... well, judge for yourselves.

First I was shown the ancient civilization of MU where now the barren sands of the Gobi desert guard the primordial secrets. Or so I thought! Later I saw the dissolution of Lemuria (were we, once, the lemuroid primates?) supposedly in or under the Pacific or the Indian Ocean. Finally I saw the mighty Atlantis, where inter-planetary travel was common for all men; yet it, too, had been swallowed beneath the turbulent waves of the Atlantic. Shall we ever be allowed to see a single iota of those past universes? No, my friend, the Gobi desert hides no secrets, the depth of the oceans does not secrete past civilizations.

Oh, they did exist—but not where we presume them to have been.

We place them in those inaccessible locations to hide them from our ineptness of not being able to locate them in our objective universe. But in the oceans of today, they don't exist; they never existed. No more than our world will exist after the end of the present procession of equinoxes. Every 52,000 years, every double grand cycle of the Zodiac, our psyche takes a gigantic leap into the unknown. The leap is so fantastic that, had we been able to retain the memories of previous experiences, our mind would not only reject them, but we would get seriously... unhinged. Perhaps stark, raving, mad.

But you don't have to worry.

When the time comes, we shall once again start at the bottom rung of the ladder. We shall enter Eden with joy in our hearts, with untrammeled faith that this, new Eden shall last forever. It almost will. Every Golden Age is by far the longest. We shall be spared the knowledge that Silver, and Bronze and the Iron Ages will follow. They don't have to, but... such is our nature.

We shall always strive to be gods, creators. Our minds shall crave knowledge even as our bodies crave physical sustenance. We shall always reach out for the stars...

But these changes will only happen when we are ready. Then the critical mass of people will make the next objective universe come into being. Yet even then, some, whose minds cannot shed archetypal memories hidden in the bottomless pit of their subconscious, shall create legends of the universes past. Some will try desperately to reach back in time. Back to an all but forgotten reality. But the critical mass, perhaps even majority of us, after eons of dabbling with the creative surges welling in our ever-expanding consciousness, shall become drunk with power. We shall come to regard the objective worlds as real universes, as worlds of substance.

And when we stray too far... an Avatar shall appear. He will remind us that the True Reality is a state of consciousness. That it exists only within our hearts. That we all, every one of us, create the ephemeral universe we live in. Some of us are proactive, some reactive, but we all take part. The Avatar will remind us that the material reality is an illusion, that it is transient; that, in time, it will dissolve itself. That it will vanish. He will remind us that the True Reality is never physical, material, but that It has its Being within the realm of the infinite potential, of inexhaustible ideas. By telling us the Truth, He will attempt to free us from our neurotic attachment to our past anchored in our own creations. We shall sense the Truth and listen to Him carefully, but the price of freedom will be too high for our egos. We would have to give up our illusory world. Our creation. So we shall crucify Him.
Just wait and see....

I wrote this essay in 1997. I could as easily have written it today. At the time, it was inspired by, who else? By Socrates. Was he an atheist? To my knowledge he didn't belong to any religion. That is why, in fact, he had been sentenced to death. Here, he is speaking to Meno:
"The soul, then, as being immortal... and having seen all

things that exist... has knowledge of them all; and it is no wonder that she should be able to call to remembrance all that she ever knew about virtue, and about everything; for as all nature is akin, and the soul has learned all things, there is no difficulty in her eliciting or as men say learning, out of a single recollection all the rest, if a man is strenuous and does not faint; for all enquiry and all learning is but recollection..."

We don't sentence our atheists to death anymore. We don't even force them to drink hemlock. Perhaps we've made some progress.

In the course of this book, I hope to prove that those invisible particles, so small that we can't see even vast quanta of them, don't really exist, either. They do but they don't. Not really. They exist only for as long as we sustain them with our minds. You'll see what I mean.

Furthermore, I also hope to prove that the reality you regarded from the moment you were a baby as real, does not really exist either. Nor do you exist, nor does your body. Nor any part of you. Nor the chair you sit on. I'll show that what the old masters were telling us is real, only they didn't have the means, the words, the metaphors to convey the knowledge that was within them.

Conversely, I'll show you what is real. Later, in the PRESENT, I'll show who you really are. And why. And... you will be amazed!

***

Chapter 6
Why We Were: Phase One

Education: A succession of eye-openers each involving the repudiation of some

THE KINDERGARTEN
(Excerpt from *Beyond Religion 1*, Essay #52)

"It begins when the rudimentary consciousness asserts its will to survive as an individual unit. An ameba, a virus, a bacterium. The mono-cellular entity becomes aware of the inside and the immediate outside of itself. It defines its territory, its boundaries. The primitive consciousness learns the laws of survival by re-embodying itself within ever more complex physical forms. Each re-embodiment is designed to increase the scope of its operations. The Sanskrit scriptures place the number of transmigrations of (each individualization of) consciousness at 8,400,000. Hopefully this number includes the second phase of our (human) evolution, though I doubt it. Suffice to say that the primary stage of our existence consists exclusively of assuring physical survival and wellbeing (through which consciousness can experience the process of becoming).

The learning process in this phase relies on repetitive conditioning. The method is that of trial and error. The repetitions serve to develop a subconscious—a storehouse of information, on which the primitive consciousness can draw to survive within its embodiment in ever changing environments. Its responses to challenges are reactive, i.e. automatic or instinctive. There is little evidence of free will or deductive reasoning; although the acquired experience is carefully stored in the genetic code of the biological constructs the entity produces to advance its evolution. At this stage, the individualized consciousness is subject to the indomitable laws of nature. A mistake costs it its life."
And nature is a very cruel mistress.

The main problem with Kindergarten is that there is no discernible communication. What little there might be, by observation only, is immediately adapted to one's own survival. Otherwise, it is ignored. This acute, purposeful self-centeredness seems to persist in some individualized unit of awareness for many eons. I know people who behave in this fashion even today, a few million years hence.

Nevertheless, nature in her wisdom has equipped our rudimentary units of intelligence with genetic memory storage, well ahead of any computer. This code carries most if not all the instructions for survival, short of the unit coming across new, unprecedented hurdles. In such circumstances, one of two things can happen. Either it follows the input from its genetic code, or, by accident or design, it tries something new. If the new works, it becomes incorporated into the revised, enhanced code, and is passed on to future generations in order to assist them in survival. I believe this is one way of looking at Darwin's "survival of the fittest," although "survival of the most resourceful" again, by accident or design, might, perhaps, be a better way to describe the Kindergarten. Nevertheless, the Kindergarten is the only phase of our evolution wherein the process of natural selection reigns supreme. Millions of years of natural selection results in a veritable plethora of most diverse, complex and beautiful organisms imaginable—not the least of which is man. Alas, at the end of the School Year, man and natural selection must part company. Thus, the learned biologists must resign themselves to deal only with primitive life forms. Unless they prefer to sit back, wait, and see what happens to their own bodies. It might prove to be a very, very long wait.

While the process of natural selection is, by definition, a process, i.e. it is not limited by time and thus it continues even today, in more advanced forms, e.g. in humans, all too often its built-in rare but necessary tendency toward mutation, turns against the organism it helped develop, by attacking the organism's immune system. The extremely prevalent rheumatoid arthritis is a well-known example of this. I suppose one could say that if it doesn't kill one, it makes one stronger. Regrettably, it takes a lot of joy out of life.

Amusing though it may seem, there are people, today, who seem motivated exclusively by the above method. They have not, as yet, taken charge of their own natural selection. They still have a 50/50 chance of survival. A little like tossing a coin. In fact I met very few people who were willing to take full responsibility for their actions. There was always someone else to blame. Perhaps, at their stage of development, they were doing the right thing.

There is one other vital lesson that we were to have learned in the Kindergarten. The lesson deals with evolutionary absolutism. It is also very pragmatic. It states quite simply: kill or be killed. You must kill to eat, thus to survive: carnivore and herbivore alike. Let us never forget that it is the same life-force that enlivens both fauna and flora. Kill or be killed is not a suggestion, it is an absolute prerequisite of natural selection.

It is unfortunate that the majority of the human species still conforms to this primitive evolutionary demand. In fact, many us don't just kill to survive, we kill because we enjoy killing. We enjoy the hunt. It seems that natural selection has not succeeded in eliminating this trait, as yet, from the human species. Will it ever?

***

Chapter 7
Atheist's Delusion

In all life one should comfort the afflicted, but verily, also, one should afflict the comfortable, and especially when they are comfortably, contentedly, even happily wrong.

John Kenneth Galbraith
Canadian-American economist and author (1908—2006)

It all started with the Democritus of Abdera, some 2400 years ago, who declares that: "Nothing exists except atoms and empty space. All else is an opinion." In his day, atoms were pictured as tiny particles, invisible and solid. Of course, in ancient Greek, *a-tomos* means indivisible, thus making atoms the smallest particles around.

This vision of reality persisted for more than two millennia. Then, all hell broke loose. At the beginning of 20th century, the physicists decided that atoms were divisible after all; that they consisted of even smaller particles. Some, a hundred thousand times smaller.

Of course, some elements have many more protons and/or neutrons than others. A carbon atom, for instance, has 6 protons and, usually 6 neutrons. Its many isotopes, however, can have from 2 to 16 neutrons. An extreme example would be roentgenium with 111 electrons, though with electrons usually contributing less than 0.06% to an atom's total mass, and some 1836 electrons needed to add up to the mass of a single proton or neutron, we needn't worry about excessive mass invading the space around the nucleus. So we can see that although the number of electrons would influence, marginally, any calculations of the total mass they might add to space surrounding the nucleus, the subatomic particles are so incredibly small that the effect on the total mass would be, I repeat, negligible. But these were just numbers, without anyone apparently trying to visualize them.

And then problems started in earnest.

Some did try to visualize them.

There were many comparisons. If the nucleus of a hydrogen atom, consisting of a proton and neutron, were to be magnified to the size of an orange, then the cloud of electrons (in case of hydrogen just one) in orbit around this nucleus would measure several miles across.

At the onset the last century, Sir Arthur Eddington, an British astrophysicist and philosopher of science, declared that, taking into account the distance between the nucleus and the orbiting electrons, atoms were mostly empty space. More precisely, he calculated that they were approximately 99.9999999999999% empty space. To wit, our bodies, the Earth, the world, all consist of atoms.

Perhaps, we might wonder, perhaps he was right. After all, surely, we all believe every word a knighted scientist would say. Always. Perhaps, to use his words, "not only is the universe stranger than we imagine, it is stranger than we can imagine." As for the electron, which has (as mentioned) 1823 times smaller mass than a proton, do we really care about them at all?

A void is a void is a void.

Thus, we are stuck with a problem. A very scientific problem, yet one about which scientists don't seem too keen to talk about.

One could say that the so-called atheists are preoccupied with 0.000000000001% of reality, which surrounds us. The rest they leave to... the 'faithful'?
Credo in unum Deum... ...factorem cœli et terræ, visibilium omnium et invisibilium.
Assuming scientists believe in the existence of atoms, they are not so far from the dictates of the Roman Church. All that is "visible and invisible". That's saying a lot about almost nothing.

Towards the end of his book Dawkins accepts the quantum reality around us, and writes that we cannot perceive the empty space of, or within, rocks, and see them only as solid, because such perception as we are equipped with, is all that's necessary for our survival; that, at least for now, we are not disposed to be able to navigate the reality of atoms. What he fails to point out is that while as animals we have sufficient perceptions to survive, we should not trust, nor draw any intellectual conclusions, from the input of our senses, as representing reality. That, regrettably, is exactly what religions of the world teach. Religions which he rejects out of hand.

Unfortunately for the scientists, the spaces between the stars, not to mention the galaxies, are proportionately even greater. You could say that the voids, of which the stars (also) consist, are separated by the astronomical voids of outer space. Thank heaven for black holes. At least they contribute a little density for the scientists to get their teeth into (although I don't recommend it, unless approved by your dentist). They, however, the scientists, seem to leave those solid jewels of the universe alone. Who knows, perhaps gods live in them?

Very, very, extremely, solid gods?

If we discount the fields of energy, then there is great probability that we, you and I, and the Earth, and the universe all around us, are essentially very EMPTY SPACE.

So much of 'physical' reality.

The fascinating thing, at least for me, is that scientists, who often base their theories on speculations, as in theoretical this-that-or-the-other, are invariably as fundamentalist in their assumptions as their counterparts in the field of theology. Since I began writing on the subject, the world had began with a big bang, invisible matter was postulated to enable the world to collapse in a big crunch, only to find, soon after, that the world continued to expand, at an ever-faster rate. This last acceleration left the scientists completely baffled.

Next to nothing, a huge mass of near empty space, speeding into the unknown nothing at astronomical velocities.

And now a word to aid the avowed atheists, who must be looking for ammunition to use against the theists, deists, and other believers in the intangible. (I feel particular indifference towards all of them—not to the people but to their views. It all seems to me to be much ado about nothing). Nevertheless this is what Jiddu Krishnamurti, of whom Henry Miller once said: "Krishnamurti is one man of our time who may be said to be a master of reality... ...I know of no living man whose thought is more inspiring."

Jiddu Krishnamurti's words:

"Your belief in God is merely an escape from your monotonous, stupid and cruel life."

Aren't we glad that we all have a wonderful life?

Mr. Dawkins' highly amusing tirade about the god of the Old Testament is based on the most fundamentalist assumptions imaginable. It is abundantly obvious that Dr. Dawkins has never heard about symbolism that is so prevalent in both, the Old and the New Testaments. Perhaps symbolism is also inherent in scientific calculations, and that is why they don't make much sense to amateurs such as I am. If so then I'm also not aware of such. So far, no scientists cared to enlighten us. Perhaps the near-empty constituents of the near-empty universe move only symbolically into the great near-empty unknown?

It's highly likely that two thousand years ago people, in order to survive in a vastly more challenging social environment, had to be vastly more intelligent. They may have been also more skilled at picking up symbolic meaning at will—except for those few who misunderstood the teaching and, as their equivalents today, were determined to destroy it.

The teaching, which had been intended solely as a means of freeing man from the constraints and limitations imposed on them by distorted precepts of Judaism, now put new noose around peoples' necks. To blame the teaching for such a turn of events would be like blaming science for the ineptitude of most scientists.

Most, not all.

In all walks of life only a few are chosen. Perhaps only a few are capable of sublimating their ego to serve humanity?

Fanatics in the ranks of religions and science are chained to their dogmas, determined to destroy each other. To blame only half of the equation will not lead us to Pragmatic Reality. As science is based on intellect and religion on emotions, I expect more from the scientist. Yet, to think that we can eliminate emotions from our life, is little more than a scientist's delusion; even as setting limits to human potential is the delusion of all atheists.

On the other hand, there is a reason why people succumb to religion, which later takes over their minds and allows priesthood to control their lives. And the reason is Darwinian absolutism. In its truest sense, Darwinian natural selection deprives people from any say in their future, in their developments. The religionists state that we are more than what nature, in her bounty, has given us; that we can make our own decisions regarding our evolution. I don't mean religion as understood by masses. They will forever (although that's a really long time) be exploited by some mental, intellectual or political oligarchy.

The dogmatism promulgated by the advocates of natural selection deprives man of any say, of any decision, in their own (forthcoming) wellbeing. Such dogmatic approach must be, and always is, balanced by some other absolutes, which might offer man freedom and assure him hope of eventual liberation. No dogma is a good dogma. At best it might be a probability, never an absolute. In this sense the Darwinian biologists sin as much as the religionists. Perhaps they ought to stick to studying lower forms of life, and leave man alone. Even religionists claim that man has freewill—even though they, admittedly, subjugate it later to their own advantage. The Darwinians don't even offer that.

The more I read Dawkins, the more I see that Darwin is god, Darwinism is a religion, and Darwinian biologists are its high priests. And if you don't fit into god's plans and his priests' dictates, then you simply don't matter. You are excommunicated. Condemned to everlasting ignorance.

In a novel *Close Call 1: Survival of the Fittist* (sic), a gentleman by the name of Randi Hacker, gives an imaginative description of a post apocalyptic world, in which a group of people turn to strict Darwinian directives. Survival is all. The consequences are not pleasant.

I recommend it to all affirmed Darwinians.

***

PART TWO — PRESENT

*"I am going to tell you what nature behaves like.
If you will simply admit that maybe she does behave like this,
you will find her a delightful, entrancing thing.
...nobody knows how it can be like that."*

Richard Phillips Feynman (speaking about quantum theory)
American physicist (1918—1988),
recipient of joint Nobel Prize in Physics in 1965.

Chapter 8
Fundamentalism in Religion and Science

Science is organized common sense—where many a beautiful theory was killed by an ugly fact.

Thomas Henry Huxley
British biologist, defender of Darwin's theory (1825—1895)

Sometime ago I read a book, which shook my faith in science. I have been attracted to it by its title: *The Elegant Universe*. It was written by a fairly well-known author of popular science books, whose ambition seems to have been to enlighten the reader, who heretofore was completely ignorant with most aspects of cosmology, physics, and particularly theoretical physics. For those who don't know, theoretical physics is a lot like religion. The scientists make assumptions, and then hope against hope that, perhaps, one day someone somewhere might confirm their speculations with 'scientific' observations. Sometimes it might work. Usually it doesn't. Just like with religions. Many religions.

Let me start by saying that I am in awe at Mr. Green's attempt to cram virtually the sum-total of human scientific achievement, as pertaining to the world we live in, into a little more then four hundred pages. A noble aim—a near-impossible task. Dr. Leon Lederman in his *The God Particle*, probably had a similar problem though he managed to include an important quote attributed to the 1979 Nobel Prize recipient in physics, Steven Weinberg, who said that: "*The more the universe seems comprehensible, the more it seems pointless.*"

So much for science?

But seriously, Brian Green put a lot of faith in his book. Regrettably, chapter after chapter, he went on to demolish the dogmas he'd presented in previous chapters. Yet, this seems to be the fate of all scientists. No sooner they establish new postulates than new discoveries demolish the previous ones. You never know where you stand. The only thing you can be fairly sure of is that all too soon someone, somewhere, will demolish whatever you'd just learned. Isn't this what happened to Einstein's dice which God was (not) rolling around the universe?

Below an excerpt from my review of *The Elegant Universe* which I posted on Amazon.com. I was really trying to be kind. Finally, I thought, finally I shall be up to date.

"I looked forward to reading this book with bated breath. At last someone who claims to know enough about Superstrings, hidden dimensions, and the final, or near-final Theory of Everything. Perhaps Feynman was wrong, after all. Perhaps Brian Green could, to use Feynman's words, '…explain it (all) to the average person.' Even if Feynman couldn't although he has 'been worth the Nobel Prize.'

I gave it a try.

The first part of the book is a fairly long-winded dissertation of the Einsteinian past. No matter, quantum mechanics would set it all right, Brian assures us. Well… it didn't. What is more, each succeeding chapter, more or less, contradicted each previous one. I know that we are just a bunch of primitives who barely scratched the slate of knowledge, but is it really necessary to fill some 400 pages with all the things that we got wrong? Don't get *me* wrong. I enjoyed it. But I have been said to be prone to mental masochism…"

This has a lot to do with, what I call, scientific fundamentalism. Each time a scientist comes up with an new idea, with a new 'observation' through their albeit myopic lenses, at least for a while such becomes a dogma. Any young scientist who'd dare to oppose the newly-arrived-at *status quo* would be 'excommunicated' from the scientific fraternity. This, by the way, was pretty much what happened to Einstein. Actually, with Einstein it went further. The Germans threw him out because he was Jewish, the French because he wasn't French, and the Americans, well, at the time, the Americans welcomed everybody, with possible exception of the Mexicans. But they came anyway.

Only later the definition of a scientific theory has changed to "a theory that has not as yet been disproven". Just as well. And that brings us to Dr. Sergio Bertolucci. Soon after he said that, "it was vital not to fool around, given the staggering implications of the result," he continues to fool around in his Laboratorio del Gran Sasso, again, with the velocity of light. Poor Albert. He lost on quantum mechanics and now...

Since his first announcement, Dr Sergio Bertolucci reported that in the second experiment neutrinos, once again, traveled through 732 kilometers of solid rock faster than light. Perhaps neutrinos know that rock is really empty space. Well, 99.999etc.etc% of it is empty space. Yet, even so, light only travels "at the speed of light" in a vacuum. On the other hand, according to Sir Arthur Eddington that seems to be virtually anywhere.

Maybe Weinberg was right.

But whatever the answer, we may be sure that other scientists will challenge it. Isn't science fun?

On the other hand, what's the point of having a theory for the sole purpose of disproving it? As Shakespeare might say, "Much ado about nothing?" Perhaps it keeps the unemployment figures down.

Nevertheless, the concept of "true until proven guilty", to paraphrase the new definition of a scientific theory, was a marked improvement on the original dogmatic approach, which originally stemmed from priesthood having a foothold in science. All theories, like all things connected with priesthood, appear to have served to help control the minds of the 'believers', although, perhaps, the 'ignoramuses' would be a better word.

On the yet another hand, once we have the Theory of Everything, who'd need God? Einstein, had he been around, would no longer want to know Her thoughts. Or, for that matter, who'd need science? We'd already know everything. EVERYTHING!

At least, in theory.

Ah, yes. In theory. We all know what the new definition of scientific theory is. Much ado…

The theoreticians, particularly the astrophysicists and their colleagues dealing with the probabilities of quantum theory, appear to have lost touch with the experimental physicists. They continued to drown us with masses of dimensions, countless universes, improbable probabilities, ever pretending that they are following a scientific method of inquiry.

It seemed to me, that to most of us, 'cosmos' means the world. To the Greeks, *kosmos* represents order, harmony, and even an ornament. Hence the world is the embodiment of a harmonious, orderly system. A thing of beauty. An ornament. What a pity that, according to our religions, such order, such harmonious beauty must come to an end. The religions have the End of the World—the scientists, the Big Crunch. Aren't they two of a kind? Why can't they both leave our world alone? And now astrophysicists are turning it upside down.

Around 1948, Fred Hoyle, Thomas Gold, Hermann Bondi and a few others, proposed the Steady State theory, also known as the Infinite Universe and/or Continuous Creation theory. In Steady State, new matter is continuously created as the universe expands, so that the Perfect Cosmological Principle is adhered to. This Principle states that the Universe is homogenous and isotropic in space and time. Or that it looks the same everywhere, the same as it always has and always will; or that the properties of the universe are the same regardless where the observer finds herself. You get the idea.

Nice, elegant solution. Beautiful, eternal, infinite. An ornament. But... no big bang, no ultimate destruction, what would the Vatican say? The atheists, who apparently form the elite of the scientific fraternity, quickly dismissed the proposal.

Yet, beauty and elegance is not an intellectual property of man. It belongs in the emotional if not spiritual realm. Most unscientific.

I recall writing an essay, some years ago, on a similar subject, entitled *Celestial and Other Bodies*, in my collection of Essays *Beyond Religion I*. Here's an excerpt.

"When an enigma occurs, the astronomers, the guys who spent all night *watching* the stars, defer to their colleagues, the theoretical physicists. Now these guys don't watch anything much, they just run a hot bath, climb in, and start thinking. Seriously, the theoretical physicists don't observe the world. They observe the observers and whenever the observers get stuck by observing or, as in this case, *not* observing what they were expecting to observe, the theoreticians start theorizing."

"Their ideas derive from an intuition about the way nature behaves on its most fundamental level, the kind of 'feeling', or hunch—almost a personal aesthetic that is every bit as important for a good theorist as the ability to solve equations."

This last observation, in italics, I borrowed from Adam Frank's article *Mystery of the Missing Star*, in the December 1996 issue of the *Discover* Magazine.

So much, once again, for the scientific method. One almost hopes for a bit of fundamentalism. The other extremes seem just as banal.

Scientific fundamentalists call their dogmas theories, but if you don't believe in them, you don't get a teaching job. You don't get to be called a professor, or become an expert on TV. On the other hand, the old adage states quite clearly that if you can't do, you teach. The question is, will anyone listen? In its most secular form, fundamentalism is a disease that restricts one's horizons. A fundamentalist tends to narrow his/her vision by looking at the world, even at pragmatic reality, solely through his or her lenses of expertise.

But one must be fair.

The church's, the Holy Roman Catholic and Apostolic Church's dogmas, with which I am more familiar, are also a matter of convenience. In my essay *Myth and Reality* (also in *Beyond Religion I*), I pointed out that the original Nicene Creed was a concise statement and included a declaration on the nature of Christ.

This Creed of the First Council of Nicaea in the year 325 has been revised at the First Council of Constantinople in 381, to settle problems raised by Arianism.

Briefly, Arianism proposed a Son who was not equal with the Father. The dispute became political with whole groups of bishops being exiled by emperors. Thus then, even as now, most 'truths' stemmed from political expediency. And let us never forget that a politician is a man, or woman, who can tell you to go to hell in such a way that you are looking forward to the trip. At least, to my knowledge, the bishops had not been excommunicated.

Much later, a 9th century addition by the Church stated

that: *'the Holy Ghost procedeth from the Father and the Son'*. This led to antagonism with the Orthodox Eastern Church.

In the meantime, the battle against Arianism continued, and in the 6th century the Catholic Church adopted a new statement. This new creed is known as the Athanasian Creed, and reinforced the belief in the Trinity and the Incarnation, which is not to be confused with *re*incarnation, which remains a no-no.

Next we come to the so-called Apostles' Creed, familiar to most conservative churches. While its origins date back to 2nd and 3rd centuries, its present form was reached in the 7th century. It is simpler than the Nicene Creed, but differs in two significant statements: it purport that Christ descended into hell, and it proposes a 'resurrection of the body', rather than the 'resurrection of the dead', avowed in the Nicene version. As Christ's descent into hell is not to be found in earlier manuscripts, the idea was probably an interpolation from the fable of Bacchus and Hercules, and adopted as an article of Christian faith.

There are other dogmatic additions. First, the dogma of papal infallibility was added in the first Vatican Council in 1870. Some years later on November 1, 1950, Pope Pius XII added the dogma of 'bodily taking up of the Virgin Mary into Heaven', which became known as the dogma of Assumption of Mary.

As long as no one questions a convenient superstition, the Church leaves it alone. The moment it is questioned, the Church declares it a dogma. Common sense is strictly against the rules.

Thus, my dear scientists, you are not alone.

Furthermore, there is little point in having a faith, a religion, or a philosophy which, although perhaps enlightening and uplifting, has no other practical application. It may be good for hermits, perhaps for advanced mystics, for the philosophers, but of little use for the billions of people who, seemingly, are walking in circles in search of some guidelines, which would keep them happy, comfortable, and healthy. Thus any proposition that one should advance to the human race should, indeed must, meet the prerequisites defined by Pragmatic Realism.

And this brings me to some such propositions. While I side with my hero (Dawkins) in rejecting Richard Swinbourne's (Emeritus Professor of Philosophy at he University of Oxford) premise that the maintenance of similarity between countless trillions of electrons calls for divine intervention, one could raise the same argument regarding the long-sought-after "Theory of Everything." Such a "Single Source" (dogma?) is normally assigned by theists to god; either that, or to covert collusion between god and theoretical physicists.

What Dawkins also fails to contemplate is that god of the Old and the New Testaments "judges no man", and thus represents a completely neutral force that could be seen as the sub-fundamental particles (think of strings of energy) possessed of infinite ability to combine and adapt their vibrations.

I, for one, regard the universe (or universes, if each originated from its own black-hole), as an example of the infinite manifested creative force. The (universal) unconscious (mind) provides the impetus for the constant supply of infinite new ideas to come, or be drawn (by the conscious mind) into the phase of becoming in the ever-forming, evolving, fulminating universes. Even as "in the fullness of time", galaxies are drawn into their individual black-holes, after whatever period of 'apostasy' (digestion, fermentation, cleansing, unwinding of complex relationship between fundamental particles, adaptation and sharing of new attributes gained over the billions of years of becoming, etc.,) the new universes come into being. Perhaps with bangs of different sizes, just to confuse the theoretical astrophysicists of the future.

Also, as mentioned in Chapter 4, I like to endow my universe with a superb if often surreptitious benevolence, rather like mentioned in the *Tao Te Ching* of Lau Tzu, or what Dawkins calls "friendly universe". Why? Because it makes me feel good and, at least in my life, I witnessed countless manifestations of it.

Forever? Why not. Providing we accept that, once and for all time, no end entails not having a beginning either. That way you don't need a god, and frankly the scientists are not of much use either. All we need is to live, and leave this, our world, our tiny ball of dust near the edge of a smallish galaxy, a better place than we found it.

That's all.

***

Chapter 9
Where We Are

The greatest mystery is not that we have been flung at random between the profusion of matter and of the stars, but that within this prison we can draw from ourselves images powerful enough to deny our nothingness.

Andre Malraux
French novelist, adventurer, art historian 1901-1976.

It is of quite unparalleled indifference to me how the world came about. The vital thing is that it did. What matters much more to me is where are we now, and where it is going, but mostly where are we now.

Oops!

Recently, we came across another problem. Someone who didn't like Albert Einstein invented Quantum Mechanics, better known as the (the already mentioned) quantum theory. While Einstein's God didn't like to play dice with the universe, the quantum physicists have no such qualms. Nothing was certain any more. The usual three dimensions, four if you count time, grew to eleven, and the single expanding or contracting universe grew to a multi-universe theory.

We may find it hard to accept, but we never lived in a universe as it really was, or is; after all, it is subject to continuous change at subatomic, atomic, planetary, galactic and, as of now, universal chance and turmoil. It, and our imaginary vision of it, must and does undergo constant change. Any scientist who claims to know what the universe really looks like is suffering from a subjective delusion, unless he's a catholic, in which case he probably received a Revelation. Sorry, sarcasm is said to be the lowest form of wit, but they (the solons of the Vatican), shouldn't have declared Fatima (read more on *Fatima* in *Beyond Religion III*) as physical reality.

The multiverse (or meta-universe etc.), is assumed by the theoretical astrophysicists to comprise everything that exists, or could exist, or ever will, would, could or might exist, including not just matter and energy but time, space and any physical laws or constants we can or cannot (as yet?) imagine. That's the pronouncement of scientists. Right—not theologians but hardnosed scientists. Of course, I don't really have any idea what sort of noses they have, except for those seeking inspirations in a bottle of good Burgundy, while lying down in a hot bath (see chapter 7, above).

Aren't we getting closer and closer to God? I repeat, these are scientists speaking, not theologians, who claim to know about God as much as the scientists know about the universe.

At least, there is a great probability that they know as much. Or not. Or that we are not in any physical universe at all? What if its all imaginary, a state of consciousness?

Hello... anyone there?

The answer to this question is becoming tougher. Presumably we are still in the universe, although we can't be sure which one. There seem to be so many scattered across the mind of God. Oops, we already eliminated God as having anything to do with, well, with anything. No problem, if we exclude God, the universes remain scattered across the minds of theoretical astrophysicists.

Let's run another bath.

Or, better still, let's start at the beginning.

We now know that we used to live in one 'universe', consisting of about 200-400 billion stars belonging to a spiral galaxy known as the Milky Way. When I was young there were only 50 billion stars populating our backyard (in the old days regarded as the only universe around). Whoever said, 'Go forth and multiply', wasn't kidding. Apparently it applied to stars, not just to people.

Assuming that we are now in one of many universes, it is good to know that even in our neck of the woods we are not alone. Our galaxy stretches some 100,000 light-years across. We are, until further notice, one of about 200 billion galaxies in the observable universe. At least that was the number counted by the astronomer Edwin Hubble around 1920s. I'm sure if anyone were to take the trouble of counting them today, there would be at least twice that number. We all multiply, remember? We, the Earthlings, are about two-thirds away from the centre of the galaxy, on the inner edge of Orion-Cygnus Arm. That's a minor spiral arm of the Milky Way, spanning only some 3,500 light years across, and stretching approximately 10,000 light years in length.

We reside on a planet orbiting, I'm sorry to say, a rather unimportant star, located in a rather unimportant place, in relatively unimportant galaxy, which we can observe only edge on, thus not seeing, or knowing, much about our galaxy at all. On the other hand, we have developed an emotional attachment to this Via Lactis, i.e. Milky Way, which some of our predecessors have affectionately called the River of Billions of Silvery Fish, and Milton referred to, in *Paradise Lost,* as "The Galaxy, that Milky Way... Powdered with Stars." Even before Milton, the ancients wondered about the expanse of stars. Below I offer some extracts from my novel *Enigma of the Second Coming*, in which Professor Hyden describes our celestial home to his daughter:

"The Anglo-Saxons of yore worshipped it as the *Waetlinga Straet*, the Street of the Giant of Waetla. It was also known to the Vikings as the Path of Odin, who was their god of gods. They called it the *Wuotanes Weg*. The Midland Dutch saw in the starry marvel the *Vronelden Straet*, the Women's Path, which seemingly lead those chosen maidens to the divine altar, with their long, snowy veils of intricate starry lacework streaming behind them. The Finns, on the other hand, saw a flock of birds migrating towards a single luminescent nest. They called it the *Linnunrata*."

"The Chinese saw in our galaxy a river teeming with silvery fish running away from the threatening hook of the crescent Moon. They called it *Tien Ho*, the Celestial River. The Hindus thought of it as the Bed of Ganges, the most holy of rivers. Lord Shiva directed the tempestuous currents of Ganges to flow through his hair and thus feed the streams of Earth. To the ancient Arabs it was *Al Nahr*, while the Hebrews thought of it as the River of Light, the *N,her di Nur*. Is that enough?"

"The ancient Polynesians scattered across the islands of the South Pacific saw in the sky a great shark consuming the clouds floating over the endless ocean. The Canadian Indians from the environs of Ottawa saw a celestial turtle roiling the muddy currents of the very same Celestial River. We took our name from the Romans. *Via Lactis* or *Via Lactea* means the Milky Way, or the Road of Milk. Possibly the North Frieslanders also reached out to Rome for their inspiration; their name of *Melkpath* speaks for itself."

"...the Greeks had many gods and goddesses. One day, Hera decided to adopt and nurse Hercules, a very, very strong mortal. In fact Hercules was so strong, that he hurt Hera's nipple, and she was forced to pull him away. Inadvertently, she spilled some of her divine breast milk. And there you have it. From these droplets arose the Milky Way. After all, Hercules was Hera's son, and Hera was the consort of Zeus, the god of gods in the Greek heaven."

"And so the Greeks called our galaxy the *Galaxias Kuklos*, meaning the Milky Band. The Romans always liked to borrow ideas from the Greeks, so they changed the name a little, to *Via Lactea*, or the Road of Milk. And that's all there is to it."

It seems that all people waxed poetic when thinking of our Milky Way. We, however, must return to the PRESENT, and be a little more scientific. Our galaxy, at 13.2 billion years, is almost as old as the universe, it is rotating around its center once every few million years, we don't know how fast, and it is also moving away from the Big Bang at a rate of between 522 to 630 km/second, depending on the relative frame of reference.

So much for our backyard.

There are other backyards. The Hubble Space Telescope estimates the number of galaxies at 125 billion. More recently, a German supercomputer simulation increased that number to 500 billion. Don't worry. Within a few years this number will grow still further. We all multiply, remember?

Closer to home—ever since Copernicus in the 16th century—we understood that Earth is just another planet. In fact, although our planet is the fifth largest in our Solar System, and measures 12,756.3 kilometers in diameter, we managed to destroy any fragment of the original Garden. Our planet still looks pretty, especially from far away, but we no longer abide in Eden. We tend to be a destructive lot, although, as already mentioned, we multiply very well. A little like vermin. When we consume everything in our vicinity, we move on to greener pastures. Albeit, we might well, soon, run out of pastures.

***

Chapter 10
What We Are

As a rule we disbelieve all the facts and theories for which we have no use. A great many people think they are thinking when they are really rearranging their prejudices.

William James,
American psychologist and philosopher
(1842—1910)

That's easy. About 99% of the human body is made up of hydrogen, oxygen and carbon. The remaining 1% consists of trace elements from dead stars, which for the purposes of our discussion, I shall ignore. (Actually, most of us are made up from elements of dead stars). Assuming an average weight of adult around 70 kilograms, that would account for some:

7,000,000,000,000,000,000,000,000,000 atoms.

[Approximately. Give or take a few billion. With my weight of 95 kilos—that's some 210 pounds for my American friends—definitely give...]

Regardless of my dietary achievements, the number of atoms is represented by a 7 followed by 27 zeros. The scientists would write it as 7^{27}. It would seem quite a handful, until we realize, as already stated in Chapter 6, that the overwhelming preponderance of the volume of each atom is empty space. Thus, this gargantuan number for which there is no name in English language, adds up to very little mass and an awful lot of void. Next time you put on a little weight, don't worry too much. It's mostly empty space.

Alternatively multiply the gain by 0.000000000001%, and have another piece of chocolate.

So... what are we, really?

Scientifically speaking, i.e. excluding mind, emotions, and of course souls, we are as much empty space as the universe that surrounds us.

Of course, the scientifically minded people will hasten to mention that the space is not empty because it is filled with wave function. Nevertheless, the total *mass* occupying space mentioned is emphatically negligible.

In spite of our size ("the mass of our physical bodies"), neutrinos have no problems with passing through the Earth, and through our bodies *en route*, without ever slowing down. Neutrinos are subatomic particles, with virtually non-existent mass, and they seem quite unaware of our presence. Perhaps we only imagine we live on Earth, whereas in fact we (see below), and the whole planet, and everything on it and in it is... just empty space.

I have one more problem with the, already mentioned, neutrinos. To recap, a neutrino (Italian for "small neutral one") is an elementary particle that usually travels close to the speed of light, is electrically neutral, and is able to pass through ordinary matter almost undisturbed. This makes neutrinos extremely difficult to detect. Neutrinos have a very small, but nonzero mass. They are denoted by the Greek letter ν (nu).

None of this bothers me. What does get my dander is that they, the neutrinos, those Italian pests, pass through me, through my body, uninvited, and without so much as leaving a card behind. We are constantly bombarded by them, and we don't even know if they'll ultimately kill us, or if they, in fact, keep us alive. Don't ask the scientists, or physicians, or priests. They're all as ignorant as I am.

But if they do give you any reasonable answer, then ask them about cosmic rays. I am told that they come from outer space and that they, too, are harmless. Like the neutrinos. Only... some of them, a very small fraction, I am told, are stable particles of... antimatter, such as positrons or antiprotons. Wikipedia assures me that the precise nature of this remaining fraction is an area of active research. Well, now. Finally I can sleep in peace! The scientists are busy researching. Theoretically, I suppose?

So much for scientific facts. You could add another million pages, but I hate writing about empty space.

It bears mentioning, that our medical profession continues to specialize in our 'physical' bodies, not realizing that they, the bodies, are not only essentially empty space, are also already dead. What is alive within us is the force that continually rebuilds our dilapidating physical envelopes, cell by cell, atom by atom. Since, the present scientific theory holds that the cells in our body are replaced every 7 years (some slow movers say 10 years, others say 14 months —as you can see this is a very precise science), I can only presume that in the intervening periods we are sort of half or three-quarters dead, depending on the rate of exchange.

The bodies we're so proud of, which many of us spend hours pumping iron in a plethora of gyms to improve, well, those bodies are mere, fragile remnants of our real selves. Our real selves are our bodies of light. In other words, life is not a biological infestations but a *process*, which wrenches order and harmony out of chaos. And if we're very lucky—beauty.

The late Eastern mystic, Sai Baba, thus described our physics or, if you prefer, our physiques:

We sit in the light.
The light is us.
We are the light.

Please note that there is no mention of spirit or any supernatural elements. He simply states that we consist of photons. In the next part, THE FUTURE, we shall argue if photons have mass. At present, photons are traditionally said to be massless. So much for our bodies.

A word about Christians. "…I am the resurrection, and the life: he that believes in me, though he were dead, yet shall he live,"(John 11:25) said the great teacher. As stated, our true body is in constant process of renewal (resurrection), and thus, our true nature is life itself.

Should we follow in Yeshûa's footsteps? Did he know something we, or our scientists, don't know—as yet? We must discover our true nature. Remember Socrates? "An unexamined life is not a life worth living." Let us examine who we are. Who we *really* are. Not the nonsense taught us by the blind who appointed themselves to lead the blind: the teachers, the politicians, the religious leaders, the pseudo philosophers, even the men aspiring to be called scientists. Don't get me wrong. Some of my best friends are scientists. Most of them are deep into probabilities. Not into dogmatic or even agnostic statements about god or their version of reality.

Let us begin to examine reality within which we find our being and our becoming. Our static and our active states.

The basic and fundamental difference between heaven and earth, between the spiritual and physical states of consciousness is that in heaven there are no consequences of our actions. (*My father—who is in heaven—judges no man*). Thus the learning process for an individualized consciousness is extremely slow. On earth, however, we pay for what we do. Or we are rewarded. We learn fast, we grow. Life on earth is an incredible gift for us—one that we ought to explore and

exploit to the maximum. Whatever we do, we cannot be indifferent, as in indifference there is no good or evil, thus there is no learning process. In indifference we are static, spiritually dead.
But that's philosophy. Or is it Pragmatic Realism?

There is another way of looking at our nature, also espoused by scientists, though of a very different kind. They also carry the title of Ph.D., as do physicists. Their particular specialty is psychology and, on occasion psychiatry.

In my book *Visualization—Creating Your Own Universe*, I wrote the following:

"The renowned Sigmund Freud is responsible for the introduction of id, ego and the superego. His model of the psyche, however, places all three components of our self within the realm of the 'unconscious'. Margaret J. Black describes Dr. Freud's primary constituents of the mind as follows:

'The id *is a cauldron full of seething excitations* of raw, unstructured, impulsive energies; the ego is a collection of regulatory functions that keep the impulses of the id under control; the superego is a set of moral values and self-critical attitudes, largely organized around internalized parental imagoes'."

This subdivision of our nature into three basic components dates back to the Bible: *Is-ra-el*, in which *Is* represents the feminine element, as well as our subconscious, *Ra*, the masculine principle or the conscious awareness, and *El*, the internal divine spark, which might correspond to the Freudian *id*, or the synthesis of the first two elements. After all, 'holy' comes from 'whole', and whole means complete.

It should be noted that Is, or Isis, is the Egyptian goddess, and Ra, the Egyptian sun-god. Furthermore, in Egyptian symbolism, Isis was often represented by a cow, suggesting Hindu influences.

It's a small world.

While Freud repudiated all religious influences, which precluded any recognition of our spiritual nature, Carl G. Jung studied and accepted the *symbolic* meaning of a number of biblical precepts. Indeed, only a fundamentalist can read the Bible *à la lettre*, thus missing the totality of the message contained therein.

Other Ph.D.'s offered more studies on similar themes. Carol Pearson suggests that we express our nature through six archetypes. Ms. Pearson borrows the concept of archetype from Carl Jung, and the concept of hero from Joseph Campbell, and evolves an interesting amalgam. Again in my book *Visualization*, the matter is discussed in much greater depth:

"...that once we leave Eden, wherein we manifested the nature of an Innocent, we will find our expression by identifying with the following archetypes: Orphan, Martyr, Wanderer, Warrior and Magician. The names of the five archetypes, somewhat suggestive of their *modus operandi*, manifest different needs, aspire towards different goals, exhibit different responses to, and methods for, overcoming problems (slaying-the-dragon), possess diverse spiritual needs, emotions, etc.. The world of each hero (that's you and me) symbolizes, and is colored by, different hues inherent in the perceptions of the various archetypes. We embody, according to Pearson, these dominating traits of character in a cyclic manner, until finally we merge the Magician again with the Innocent, our place of origin, only to eventually leave Paradise once more in search of new adventures."

In addition to references given above, anyone who wishes to discuss the matter of "what we are" further, I offer my essay *Organized Matter*, from my collection of essays *Beyond Religion II* and *Self*, in *Beyond Religion I*, both published on Amazon and Smashwords. The matter is also discussed in depth in the chapter *Redefining Self*, in my book *Visualization—Creating Your Own Universe.*

That only leaves the avowed 'believers'. The 'faithful'. Now I don't give a bag of bones if you decide that you are a bag of bones. But about a billion Christians, a comparative number of Moslem, believe that they possess soul, and even more Hindus believe in atma, which is best translated as soul. Thus, like it or not, we must examine the concept.

Soul is the most mistranslated word in the Bible. Most times, the Hebrew word *nephesh* is translated as soul. The true or correct translation is "animal soul", or that attribute of our body, which keeps us physically alive. You might call it ego, which is necessary for physical survival. The most powerful aspect of *nephesh* is the survival instinct. *Nephesh* also corresponds to our subconscious, which is a storehouse of information since the instant of first awareness. Every animal is endowed with it; it is that which causes us to feed, to hunt, to procreate and to do all we can to assure our physical survival. However, note that animals do not hunt for the future. They eat as much as they can and refrain from hunting until hunger motivates them to start looking for food once again.

Not so man. Man, speaking generically, i.e. both men and women, are not satisfied with a full stomach. We, tend to amass extra food both, in our stomachs and our fridges. What we cannot fit there, we put in the banks, in the form of eventual food, presumably to maintain our status of the most obese species in human history. Of the world? Survival of the least-fit? Darwin would turn in his grave. No matter how Christians we profess to be, we choose to ignore the biblical admonition, "Take no thought for your life, what ye shall eat, or what ye shall drink; nor yet for your body, what ye shall put on. Is not the life more than meat, and the body than raiment?" It seems the only admonition that reached our ears is about *what ye shall put on*. We put on *weight* without any worry. In the USA, at least 65% of us do. In Germany, 75.4%

succeed in not worrying either.

The answer, therefore, to the biblical admonition is a definite, profound NO. Forget it. What do you know? Not for Christians nor, from what I gather, for most other people of whatever persuasion. Yes, including the avowed atheists. Of course, they are under no obligation to learn anything from the evangelists. They can make up their own rules on how to get fat.

Evidently we do not feel that life is more than food, and our body more than raiment. A bag of bones? We, the incredible preponderance of us, most definitely regard ourselves as our body, which might, perhaps, be endowed with a 'soul'. Judging by our behavior, it is most emphatically an 'animal soul'.

This assertion, in turn, makes us most definitely animals. Now, at last, we know what we THINK we are.

There is absolutely nothing wrong with being an animal. Some of my best friends are animals. If, by your behavior and belief you indicate that you are one, then allow me to assure you that I love animals. Really. I love animals, including some human ones. Unfortunately, the man credited with the philosophy expressed by the New Testament, calls all who regard themselves as such: "dead". Remember? "Let the dead bury the dead". So why do we think that we are alive? Well, because life is a manifestation of change, and we (as do all other animals) do change. So we are half-right, anyway.

Physical reality, including our physical bodies, can be compared to ashes left after the fire used up their usefulness. Our real universe, our real bodies are bundles of energy, held together by the act of our will. As Evelyn, M. Monahan (*The Miracle of Metaphysical Healing*) once said, "our will is the most powerful force in the universe." Or, I strongly suspect, in any reality.

Or, we can detach ourselves from our bodies and regard ourselves from without. As though in a mirror. We might

DELUSIONS

learn that we are in a constant process of recreating ourselves in an endless procession of images. It is not easy. But, if we are to believe Krishnamurti: "The image that (my) thought has created is 'me'. The 'me' is the image. There is no difference between 'me' and the image."
I am *that* I am.

Life is only the memory of a dream.
It comes from no visible rain.
It falls into no recognizable sea.

Sai Baba

There is one other item to consider. We have been described (by a scientist whose name I can't remember) as mobile robots, designed for the sole purpose of providing food for our genes, to keep them immortal. This includes our ability to reproduce in ever increasing numbers. But there is one other item that particular gentleman hasn't considered.

Deep within us, in the dark dungeons of our stomachs and other internal organs, there is a plethora of life the biologists don't seem to like to consider.

There are about 50 trillion (some sources report as few as 10 trillion) cells in a human body. It sound like a lot but it pales in relation to the number of bacteria who/which makes their home in/on us.

Let us start with the proposition that there are ten times as many bacteria in the human body as there are cells. That comes to at least 100 trillion, or 10^{14}. That's 100 followed by 12 zeros. Take your pick.

Now, rather then imagining that we are mobile robots designed for the sole purpose of sustaining the immortality of our genes, how about redefining the function which the robots have, not instead of, but in addition to their primary function. What if the real purpose of human body is to keep the bacteria alive? Life is life. Bacteria are people too, aren't they?

The bacteria send us out to pasture, they keep us alive, they multiply like crazy (I wonder where they got that idea), and finally they continue their enjoyable existence on our children and our children's children. Sometimes, in the process of their own reproduction they destroy the internal mechanism of the 'human' cells, but, well, we can't all have everything, can we?

There is another tidbit for J. Craig Venter *(A Life Decoded)*. A great number of the bacteria occupying the best real estate in our body are anaerobic. They don't need him to crate earth-like conditions on other planets to survive. They can do very nicely without oxygen, thank you.

On the other hand, if bacteria find it profitable, I wouldn't be at all surprised if they were already working on converting some planets in the universe to sustain the biological life of the best milking cows they ever found. There. We all have a noble purpose. Or, perhaps we are more than feed-bags? I leave that to the atheists to cogitate. I am told that the human brain is not immune to bacterial invasion.

***

Chapter 11
The God Diffusion

*All gods are homemade, and it is we who pull their strings,
and so, give them the power to pull ours.*

Aldous Leonard Huxley,
British author (1894—1963)

In the West, we like to rely on scriptural statements taken verbatim from the Bible. There are, however some 6 billion people who do not share our views. The non-Christians have their own problems to solve.

In her book on esoteric Buddhism, *The Secret Doctrine*, which Einstein is said to have kept on his bedside table, Helena Petrovna Blavatsky shares with us dogmas, or theories, of quite a different kind. They are derived from the life of Brahma, the god of creation. A kalpa is a single day in the life of Brahma. Two kalpas are a day and a night. Each kalpa is composed of 1,000 Maha Yugas. And this period is amazingly close to the life of planet earth.

The scientists tell us that the oldest rocks which have been found on Earth date back to about 3.9 billion year ago. However, those rocks include some minerals, which are as old as 4.2 billion years.

Now... guess what.

A kalpa is therefore equal to 4.32 billion human years.

Coincidence?

But don't worry. If they are both right, the esoteric

Buddhists and the scientists, then we still have about 120 million years left, before Brahma wakes up and a new order of things begin.

But let us stick to Maha Yuga and its characteristics.

First, esoteric Buddhism does not take physical evolution into account. In fact they define our existence as continuous *devolution*, lasting some 4,320,000 years, and which period is called Maha Yuga (or the Great Year). Each such Yuga is divided into four Ages, whose lengths follow the ratio of 4:3:2:1. As the gods of the East appear kinder to us than the gods of the Near East, the longest of these Ages is the Golden Age, the shortest is the present, or the Iron Age, known also as Kali Yuga. Of one thing we can be sure: we're on the way out.

In her book, the late H. P. Blavatsky took it upon herself to decipher ancient writings hidden in the upper reaches of Tibet. Her findings are discussed in my book *Visualization— Creating Your Own Universe*. I quote some (gently edited) parts:

"The myths embrace the Atlanteans, the Lemurians, and reach further back as though in a blink of an eye. Time is nothing to Theosophy, as indeed it seems like nothing to all who have read it. In the midst of all this, HPB (as Ms. Blavatsky was known to her colleagues) stresses the reality of the present. No mean achievement.

The Theosophical cosmogony also revolves in cycles. Yet they (the cycles) do not strike me as truly repetitive. From the mists of prehistory, reaching back countless millions of years, the humanity evolves in a series of Root-Races. They are seven in number and now we have reached the middle of the fifth Root-Race, which became established *su generis* approximately a million years ago. Each Root-Race is in turn divided into seven Sub-Races, which, in turn, are composed of seven Family-Races. This last subdivision has a life-span of some 30,000 earth-years, and is made up of innumerable tribes and nations lasting some 4,000 to 5,000 years each."

"Each Root-Race goes through repetitive cycles of Golden, Silver, Bronze and Iron Ages. The subgroups echo this rotation, rather as in the Hindu mythology, but the subdivisions allow for a greater awareness of present conditions. In Theosophy, after the Age of Kali, steeped in materiality, we know that a new Satya Yuga (the new Golden Age) is just around the corner. The corner might spell a few thousand years of waiting, but presents a more rewarding prospect than global dissolution, with which the Jews, the Christians, the Moslems, and the scientists are so enamored. And if we are prepared to settle for latter rewards, then, with a dose of optimism, we can devise a sub-sub-cycle, which will place us in a mini-age of Silver or Gold sub-age often enough to combat an ongoing bout with manic depression.

A broader view is more pessimistic. We have only just completed the first 5,000 years of the Iron Age cycle of Kali Yuga, which began with the death of Krishna. In terms of mega-cycles, we have a long wait for the new Golden Age. I am grateful that my own thoughts have evolved along the lines that we all create our subjective realities, no matter how illusory, and my own reality seldom strays far from the golden hues.

A word about our past.

In Theosophy, we had not been created by God in Eden, or any other specific location, but rather we result from the cooperation between Nature and Higher Beings. Nature took us as far as she could along the upward path, and then gods granted us the mind, which facilitated continued struggle. As for the distant future, we have two more Root-Races to go, before we join our Hindu friends and cease to be. Rather like in a Big Crunch, which, as mentioned, our astrophysicists are determined to impose on us. As for the timing, don't hold your breath, the present Iron Age, the Kali Yuga, still has some 417,000 years to go. Give or take a few thousand.

That's the bad news or the good news, depending whether you enjoy your life in Kali Yuga. The other good or bad news is that each Family-Race more or less disappears every 30,000 years, a mere blink of the cosmic eye. Strangely enough the tectonic plate movements, the periodic shifting of the earth's magnetic poles, and the unexpected bombardment from our asteroid belt could easily accelerate this schedule. So—maybe we shouldn't take any deep breaths, after all."

The Hindu vision is truly cosmogonic.

"To clarify, its ancient brush paints a more disturbing picture. While the Jains (people who follow Jainism) offer a cycle in which there is also an upward trend toward self-betterment, the Hindus deny us this relief. They start, as do the Jains, at the very top, in the glorious Golden Age, Satya Yuga (more accurately—the Age of Truth). This age of bliss and beauty is by far the longest of the four ages of the Maha Yuga, and lasts 1,728,000 years. I would suggest it is equivalent to the period humanity had spent in Eden. It is followed by the Silver Age during which we are still blessed with considerable virtue and beauty for the next 1,296,000 years. Then things begin to deteriorate more rapidly. We lose a lot of our spiritual values and seem to straddle the ethical fence. This Bronze Age lasts for 864,000 years. Mercifully, the last Age, in which humanity sinks to the lowest level and is steeped in materiality and egotism, is shortened to 432,000 years only. It is appropriately called the Iron Age, the least noble of the four metals. As stated above, another name for this period is Kali Yuga—variously translated as "age of vice" or "age of the male demon Kali", a little strange since Kali is (also?) a Great Hindu Goddess."

The ancients, you'll note, had not been concerned with our bodies, or with our civilizations, but with the development, or otherwise, of our Atma. If you are a scientist living in India, you face completely different problems than scientists swimming the ocean of Christianity. I wonder if the

Hindu scientists also worry so much about god, and or other divinities, as the western scholars seem to. If so, my condolences.

It is vital that we understand the essence of this teaching. There are many ways to interpret devolution. The ancients were thinking in terms of spiritual entities, or beings, gradually sinking into materiality. In this process we were intended to learn and develop individuality. Perhaps nature or other universal forces are grooming us to take over various worlds, in which scientists will spend their lives trying to prove that we don't exist.

No matter, as long as they are having fun.

Regardless of the imminent and apparently unavoidable devolution, it is my contentions that some individuals, few and far between, would swim against the current (the chosen few) and would indeed rise up to unprecedented heights, while the vast majority would succumb to their inevitable nadir, only to begin again in another megacycle. This, according to the eastern philosophies, or as Blavatsky prefers to call 'theosophies', takes place over many millennia, or as already mentioned, some 4,320,000 years. Although on mega-scale the only concern is the descent of man from spiritual to material consciousness, the cycles within cycles, contrary to the laws of natural selection, also speak of degradation of physical faculties of survival.

On a minute scale, a simple example of the latter comes to mind. Imagine dropping a primitive man in the middle of a Brazilian jungle, with but a pocketknife in hand. The man would have a good chance of survival for an extended period, probably a number of years. Then, 100 miles away, drop a Wall Street executive similarly armed. I wouldn't give him a week. That's what I mean by physical devolution.

There are other illustrations.

Perhaps because I am convinced that the ancient sages of the East were right in their prognostications of reverse evolution, of foreseeing that even as material goods and comforts grow they pull us away from our true nature, from our higher consciousness, I have been called an iconoclast. Yet I only expose the folly of that which holds us back from developing our true potential. And make no mistake about it. We are drifting away.

It is hard to define the direction humanity has chosen to espouse. Here's but one example.

A great deal has been said about the complexity of characters in the book "*The Girl with the Dragon Tattoo*". A story about (inter alia) a misogynistic avenger. The fact remains that the story raises our taste for depravity, our penchant for our lowest instincts, and our propensity towards sadism, to an altogether new low level. And that book, and many like it, sates our emotional needs, infiltrates our character by osmosis. To the day of writing these words, the book has sold 65,000,000 copies. Did those 65 million people know what they were buying? Or have we already developed a sense of sniffing out the lowest level that will gratify our needs in advance.

While there are a number of 'oldies' bestsellers, which will never be caught, among them the Bible, the Bhagavad-Gita, and the Qur'an—which are the most-printed books ever—they also share the dubious privilege of being the most maligned and most ridiculed books by most atheists, who never took the trouble to even attempt to understand them.

Fundamentalists hate competition.

In addition to the 'literature', the meaning of which has changes substantially since a good dose of sadism, mayhem and murder became its mandatory ingredients, (sorry Mr. Shakespeare, at least you did it with such poetic charm), there is also Hollywood—the USA single biggest exporter—the Americans' cultural gift to the world. More often than not, the prerequisite of a successful film (movie) is an avalanche of corpses splattered in great many likely and unlikely places. Unless you see dozens of policemen with guns drawn, held threateningly in both hands, you haven't enjoyed yourself. Or

so, apparently, the public thinks. Or else, this is the opinion the Hollywood morons, sorry, I meant solons, have of their public.
Are they right?
Hardly. I just heard that Meryl Streep has been acclaimed as the greatest actress of all time. Yet, lo and behold, I do not recall (with forgivable exception of *Sophie's Choice*) any corpses adorning any of her films. In spite of that, all her films are financial successes. Could it be that she can really act?
She is one of the chosen few.
We, *en mass*, are definitely devolving. Fast.

Few people realize that there is a parallel philosophy suspended between the Hindu and the Hebrew traditions, hidden in the Bible. The golden age can be compared to the period the human consciousness had spent in Eden. Then, there followed a period of inordinate longevities, exemplified by a number of people. For those interested, I discussed the matter briefly in my book *Visualization—Creating Your Own Universe*.

If we are to take the Biblical information scientifically (or literally as a good fundamentalist would), then we can broadly divide the long living ancients into two groups—those living before and after the flood. The average life span before the flood (some ten generations) has been calculated at 857 years. After the flood, the average life span of also some ten generations (from Shem to Abraham) has shrunk to a mere 317 years. A considerable difference. It should be noted that in biblical symbolism (see my *Dictionary*) moving water normally represents great changes in consciousness.

Examples of the first, or the pre-flood group, which corresponds (symbolically) to the Silver Age in Blavatsky's *The Secret Doctrine*, would include Methuselah, boasting 969 years, Jared 962, Noah 950, Seth 912, Kenan (Cainan) 910,

Enos, 905, Mahalalel 895, and Lamech 777. Some include Adam and Eve in this group, although we have no knowledge how long they stayed in Eden before they were given 'skins', which represents (to me) the onset of the Silver Age.

Examples of the second group, living *after* the great flood, with considerably shorter life-spans, and again, representing symbolically the Bronze Age, would include Shem 600, Eber 464, Terah 205, Abraham 175, and Moses, who is said to have lived 120. And all this without the benefits of Medicare.

The average age before and after the great flood differs substantially.

I would, again, suggest that these periods corresponds in Hindu mythology's Silver and Bronze Ages, although how the knowledge of such correspondence between the Bible and esoteric Buddhism occurred remains a mystery.

The present, evidently extremely materialistic Age, must belong in the Iron or Kali category. Of course, there is considerable disparity between the overall duration of each period. Alas, time in metaphysics is extremely flexible.

Below, once again, an excerpt from my book *Visualization*, the Chapter on *Aging and Longevity*, which discusses, *inter alia*, the flexibility of time.

"The concept of flexibility of time is not new. St. Thomas Aquinas proposed three types of time. *Tempus* concerned the 'temporal' or earthly time. It measured the duration of changes taking place on earth. The second type of time Aquinas called *aevum* or time affecting changes in or of mental processes. It did not concern material changes but rather changes in mental states. It also applied to all that is incorporeal, to angels and to states of consciousness. The third type of time Aquinas called the *aeternitas*. It concerned the divine. While it was the domain of God, it also embraced our ability to experience infinity or immortality in a single instant. It is the time that permits the present and infinity to

DELUSIONS   103

be one.

   In science, Aristotle and Newton measured time unambiguously as the duration between two events. They believed it was *absolute time*. Then, Einstein destroyed the misconception that time is absolute. In his theory of relativity he married the concept of time and space into a single idea of space-time. According to the physicist Stephen Hawking, the distinction between space and time disappears completely when using *imaginary time*; time measured using imaginary numbers. There is no difference between going forward or backward in imaginary time. We can also go in any direction in space. Other scientists took up the banner and came up with different definitions of time responding to different qualities and/or events of past, present and future. Another Professor of mathematical physics, Frank Tipler, offers us an elaborate menu of different 'times'. He measures duration in terms of *proper time*, as measured by our clocks in the present astrophysical environment. Using this definition, time and space is measured in the same units, i.e. if time is measured in years then distance is measured in light years. He also computes in *conformal time*, which is measured in terms of a specific scale factor. We don't have to worry about it because, as far as I understand, it is used only to calculate the behavior of light rays. Then there is the *entropic time*, which "is a more physically significant time-scale than *proper time*." It is used to measure the amount of entropy that exists in the universe at a specific proper time. Next is the *subjective time* defined as the time required to store irreversibly one bit of information. Rather as in the speeds of computers. Finally the theoretical physicists use the *York time*, so called after the American physicist James York, which simplifies mathematics of the field equations."

   Quite a choice...
   Over the years, the whole concept of time underwent considerable adjustment. In John 8:58 Jesus says, "*before*

Abraham was, I Am". I'd suggest that he was referring to his state of consciousness, not his physical, or biological envelope.

I would further suggest to you that if we define our world in terms of mass and energy, then a statement *"before the world* was, *I am,"* would make equal sense. In metaphysical terms, consciousness must exist *before* its manifestation can be embodied in any physical or even quasi-physical form, even as an idea must exist before we can begin thinking about it, ignite it with the fervour of emotions, and begin to bring it out into physical manifestation. As is the case with this book.

Just think. As I write this on my computer, the book is being constructed entirely of photons. Entirely of light. Just think of that.

***

Chapter 12
The End of the Beginning

Politics is not the art of the possible. It consists in choosing between the disastrous and the unpalatable.

John Kenneth Galbraith
Canadian-American economist and author, (1908—2006)

From the point of view of esoteric Buddhism, the USA, being by far the most successful nation from the strictly materialistic wealth point of view, is also the closest to having reached its nadir. By definition, economic success equates with materialism. This includes the supposed bastions of spiritual life, wherein the TV preachers seem never tired of filling their deep pockets with poor peoples' money. Poor people who are seeking solace. There is ample evidence to back up this observation.

Then there is the secular aspect.

Most, if not all inventions that facilitate the so-called quality of life are intended and produced for lazy people. What made the USA so rich had been principally the ability, willingness, and the acumen of the few to exploit this amazing desire for laziness and mental inertia of the many. This mental malaise is evident in the vast majority of its citizens. The actual inventors are the few and far between individuals who actually enjoy intellectual challenge. Yet...

without the market on which to unload their ideas, they would die of starvation, or, at the very least, they would not become billionaires.

Before looking down our noses at others, assuming that was ever the case, let me state right here that I, too, suffer from symptoms of laziness. I am writing this book using a wonderful labour saving device known as MacBook Pro, referred to affectionately as the Macintosh. I could use a quill or a pen, but, well, I am lazy. Also, I can work 5-6 times faster, thus not lose my train or thoughts, and later do my preliminary editing without having to rewrite hundreds of pages. There is a difference though. While I admit to being lazy, the use of the genius of the few, in my case Messrs. Jobs and Wozniak, enabled me to write more than thirty (yes, 30) books since I retired from my profession. Not much, but it's the best excuse I can offer.

For the moment, let us leave the few and return to the many, to the masses—to the silent majority, which of late is becoming more vocal.

It should be made clear that genius and hard work alone does not, necessarily yield stellar financial rewards; although it has been said that genius is 5% talent and 95% sweat. It does, on occasion, though. Once again, I have Steve Jobs in mind. But he's one of the few exceptions. One can also become rich by cheating, stealing, lying, and indulging in political games and abuses. I am told that all, or nearly all, members of the Senate *and* the House of Representatives in the USA are said to be multimillionaires. In Britain, David Cameron's coalition Government is said to be run by a £60million Cabinet. 23 of the 29 ministers entitled to attend Cabinet meetings are estimated to have assets and investments of more than £1million. Not much by American standards, but it's a start.

There are many ways to skin a cat, and there is hope.

It seems that natural selection appears to take care of such mutant products of its evolution, and the abusers, if such they are, will eventually pay for their misdeeds. They will no longer be elected to their illustrious offices; they will be imprisoned for genocidal acts; or they will be rejected by society, which will eventually become aware of their vile characters. In the East, this is called the workings of Karma. Here, in the West, we say that justice has long memory and long arms, though sometimes the memory seems to try our patience. Both concepts work in a pragmatic sense.

There are those who claim that only a small percentage of those caught are punished, and even fewer are caught. Since many share the views of the accusers, this may have been why at the beginning of this chapter I mentioned esoteric Buddhism and Karma. And since particularly the members of the Republican Party and their henchmen never fail to quote the Bible, let me add a few reminders:

"Whatsoever a man soweth, that shall he also reap." *Galatians (6:7)*
"For verily I say unto you, Till heaven and earth pass, one jot or one tittle shall in no wise pass from the law, till all be fulfilled." *Matthew (5:18)*
"And it is easier for heaven and earth to pass, than one tittle of the law to fail." *Luke (16:17)*

Neither Karma nor the Law have any statutes of limitations on any crimes. And punishments can be extracted in many different ways. Perhaps by nature herself.

But what really destroys any organized society is greed, and greed is usually the direct result of envy. Keeping up with the Jones's is the mildest symptom of this, affecting even the disaffected masses. Usually, the malaise goes much deeper. In my essay *The Green Eyed Monster*, I recounted a little story, and later I shall offer a few examples to show that even the scientists are not immune from this disease. Here's brief excerpt.

"I am reminded of a story I heard from a kindly old man. He said he had a vision of Hell. He saw a dark place filled with great cauldrons wherein the perpetrators of various crimes were slowly stewed in their own oil. Devils, armed with barbed tridents, surrounded virtually all the cauldrons. They pushed back the sinners who were struggling to escape their just deserts back into the simmering oil. All cauldrons with the exception of one. The pool filled with those who committed the sin of envy needed no guards. The other fryees pulled the aspiring escapees back into the oil themselves."

Such is the nature of envy.

Now, a word about her sister—greed. (or 'brother', just to be politically correct). Greed is defined, inter alia, as intense desire for wealth, power or fame.

Most of us associate greed with financial dealings— the multi-million bonuses being the best example of this. There is also the presumed benefit of the resultant power—as in political ambition, or a prestigious position—as in grossly overpaid and 'over-bonused' CEOs, who consider themselves much, much "more equal than the others". To these people we must add the Hollywood conclave who get paid many millions of dollars, sometimes for little more than stripping in front of a camera, or pretending to kill people with a plethora of weapons starting with knives, pistols or weapons of semi-mass destruction, like machineguns, dynamite or other explosives, all to amuse the young and impressionable minds, who henceforth dream of following in their idols' footsteps. It is a strange world we live in when a third-rate actor in a third-rate sitcom is earning 10x more than a neurosurgeon.

Finally we must add to the entertainment industry the professional sportsman and sportswomen, pumped full of performance-enhancing drugs who, seemingly, would do almost anything to be signed up for a few extra million dollars in their contract.

This select group is followed by thousands of 'hungers-on', agents, sleazy physicians who supply the drugs, overambitious trainers, go-betweens, political pollsters, and an army of other, lesser greed-mongers, who together comprise a nation at the end of its world domination. By now one might change the government, but the malaise is set too deep to be eradicated from above. Soon it will be time to start again, at the beginning.

As for peoples' greed for power, I read somewhere that only a fool would want to be the president of the USA—only a saint would agree to be one. Somehow, watching various primaries over the years, try as I might, I could not detect any symptoms of sainthood. Perhaps this was just me.

To be fair to the USA, as of writing this chapter, Italy was in the throes of an austerity program. Their politicians, however, were paying themselves about twice the European governmental average. Bravo Berlusconi!

This malaise may have infiltrated also the lower financial levels of the society but, due to lack of power and influence, members of this group are more likely to hurt themselves than others.

With the collapse of the trustworthiness of the media, there remain a few brilliant exceptions. A wise man by the name David Brooks, a columnist for the New York Times, is one of them. He said that the "American socioeconomic system was built on trust." He was speaking of the past. The consequence of greed and corruption is loss of trust. A hermit does not rely on it, but when two or three meet, trust becomes *sine qua non*. And the American system has been built on cooperation.

Now imagine 7 billion people who don't trust each other... The latest consequence of this malaise is that people, the world over, no longer trust their governments. If greed and corruption in the western world might spell economic disaster, the pandemic threatens humanity.

Is there hope?

Pragmatic Realism demands strict ethical standards. If a

person's indomitable will to achieve is not tempered by humility, sooner or later greed will show its ugly head. Do you know many successful people who are humble?

As for envy, greed's younger sister (again, brother for avowed feminists, although diamonds are said to be girls' best friends), its insidious influence is not limited to business, politics, big business or the entertainment/sports industry. It is not even limited to egos suffering from obscurity. Another example from my essay referred to above.

"Thomas Alva Edison held over 1300 patents. His accomplishments evidently led to such an inflated ego that he fell under the spell of envy. At one time, rather then offer congratulations, he preferred to destroy the reputation of Nikola Tesla, by spreading garrulous nonsense about the dangers of his competitor's invention—that of electric alternating-current (A/C). He laid nonsensical claims as to the efficacy of his own discovery, the direct-current (D/C), though he was already well aware of its limitations. In time Tesla was well and truly vindicated, but not before Edison drove him to near bankruptcy by his envy."

Tesla, in turn, condemned Albert Einstein's early achievements out of hand, without ever giving them the benefit of the doubt, let alone a serious study."

Ain't we got fun? And these were scientists!

For readers interested in the subject, there is more, much more, in my essay. But... it's not very pleasant to read.

The USA only declared its independence on July 4, 1776, yet, all too soon, it reached the end of its beginning. Each successive empire, be it political, military or economical, lasts a shorter time. What destroys it is greed. The Declaration of Independence of 1776 was probably the most wonderful document ever written. In ancient history, some empires lasted many centuries. America has already reached the End of its Beginning. Wouldn't it be a shame if the American hegemony also reached the Beginning of its End?

As of the date of writing this book, the democracy in the USA was dead. It existed only among the rich. The very rich respected each other. They held the masses in deep disdain. The media did not report the truth. They, too, were in the pockets of the wealthy ruling class. They were little people with inflated egos who knew so very little, yet were telling the masses about so much. The blind leading the blind.

There were exceptions—few and far between.

Yet, within this quagmire of greed and envy, there were two unique, and diametrically opposing rays of hope. The first was the philanthropic movement started by billionaires. Strangely enough, those who derived the greatest benefits from the action often resided outside American borders. Nevertheless, if this wonderful idea were to catch fire among the 'ordinary' men and women, we might have to ask not how much the rich had given, but how much they had left. And then, perhaps, the masses would give also.

The second ray of hope might have far greater repercussions.

Recently a movement has started, first among the Arab countries, then among the Europeans, and finally in the USA. It appears that very ordinary people—those who have never been consumed by the contagion of greed—raised their heads. They grew fed up with dictators, be they political, economical or of any other sort. At least closer to home the protesters, as they chose to be called, didn't shoot, didn't fire guns—unless someone shot at them, they didn't make demands on anyone or anything. They just said that they were fed up with the greedy plutocrats who were stealing their hard-earned keep. They said that the greedy ones must find a solution. It's their job. They stole, robbed the middle class, the masses, they must find a way to return all stolen goods. The stolen money. Trillions upon trillions of dollars. They, the protesters, were a quiet, almost humble lot of people, who normally didn't complain.

The strange thing was that, to start with, even the media didn't take them seriously. The quiet protesters were not newsworthy. They were too quiet. They didn't burn cars or destroy property. They were nice people. And the media were... in the pockets of the very rich. They destroyed, twisted the truth, or simply ignored it. They, too, would have to go. Permanently. Together with the devils they served so obediently.

For people who study such social fermentations, these quiet, pensive upheavals were merely just another expression of the Age of Aquarius. It is the Age in which we would, in which everyone *must* learn, to water his and her own garden. To stand up on our own feet. The atheists must find their own explanations. I hope they will not blame Darwin.

But one thing is certain. Unless the people, yes, the ordinary people, succeed in tearing down the Corporate America, the USA and all the glorious ideals it stood for will collapse sooner than anyone dared imagine. I single out America, but the whole Western world must be included. We all share in the guilt.

As for the scourge of unemployment, one look at the Plaza di St. Marco, in Venice, would show clearly why the Doges never had to face the problem of unemployment. Quality requires work. And work requires manpower, with the accent on *man*. Just look at those facades! Shall mankind ever forsake quantity for quality? Quantity is the prerogative of natural selection—we must rise higher. Some of us need two or three automobiles, two or three houses, two or three boats, four or five TVs, and five or six millions of dollars in the bank. Are we past the point of no return?

Or are we too decadent already?

Old America is dying. New—has not been, as yet, defined.

And then, there is also the political angle. In Pragmatic Realism one is forced to search for the most practical solution to all problems, including the nation's problems. In the USA, the triumvirate of power: the Executive, the Senate and the House of Representatives, have only one purpose. *To find best solutions to serve their country.* Of late, this function, this purpose, was not evident from their actions, or lack of actions. Of late, they did not represent the people. They represented the financiers who, *inter alia*, according to the 60 Minutes CBC (CBS in the USA) news program aired in November 2011, enabled the members of both houses to indulge in the highly illegal insider trading. It appears that the honorable members are running short on honor.

The Hegelian solution is fairly simple. To adapt it to the political sphere, there ought to be a thesis and antithesis, the marriage of which results in the best possible synthesis. This is no longer so. Nobody seems to care what is right, only who wins the argument. This places the opposing parties at an impasse. Let us hope that the juvenile behaviour of all parties heralds the End of the Beginning. Not the Beginning of the End. Let us hope, that soon the overpaid politicians will come of age.

A phrase comes to mind: "A house divided unto itself cannot stand." While the biblical words deal with the state of consciousness of an individual person, the political echo is self-evident. As for the 'Spring', be it in the Arab countries, in Europe or on the States, it seems to me that a nation divided on 93%-7% wealth allocation cannot stand either.

Alas, there is hope of late, in 'ordinary' peoples' awakening. Is hope a prerequisite of science? I see little evidence of it. The best I have observed is that the omnipresent rise of visual communication makes it harder for the oligarchy to use their henchmen, the police, the army, and other law-enforcing agencies, to intimidate and abuse people seeking for justice. A single strike, clout or punch, or any act of physical violence by any other name, delivered by a cold-blooded brute dressed in blue or khaki uniform, is seen, examined, and condemned all around the world instantly. It is displayed the world over, at the velocity of light. We have science, the exponential growth of technology, to thank for that.

We also have this technology to thank for making us all aware of the degree of corruption that saturates the very top of society of virtually all nations. This insidious corruption now begins to trickle down to infest lower levels of society, and to trickle down even as water does, to eventually find its lowest level. Our time gives ample testimony to the maxim that power corrupts. We have also learned by this process that sadism, bullying, taking advantage of the weaker, is not limited to any one nation. It is a universal malaise. It differs only in degrees to which it is applied. It is an omen of devolution.

The Beginning of the End? Or just a symptom of the Age of Kali?

Nevertheless, it is this communication technology enhanced by the courage displayed by the participants in the Spring of Nations that might yet bring back the social, economic, and political factions from the brink of annihilation. At present we, virtually the whole world, is hovering over the precipice. It certainly is the end of our childhood.

And what of science? Will our scientists finally come of age? Or will they continue to dip their fingers and our dollars to examine the past, the long dead corpses of what once was? Should we really spend millions of dollars of *public* money to study paleontological bones when live bodies need medical attention? Isn't it time to face the facts and admit that we not only don't know what we once might have been, but that we have little idea of what we are today? Here and now?

Shouldn't we begin to live in the Present?

Regrettably, it seems to me that we shouldn't hold our breaths. Just as recently the same scientists (or their cousins?) while attempting to find the "Theory of Everything" had already proven that they cannot prove anything. That's right. That there are no absolutes. We had a foretaste of it in the Theory of Relativity. Everything was, still is, relative. But at least some things were definitely relative to each other. Definitely relative, as in "we're relatively ignorant about who we are, where we are, let alone why we are wherever it is that we are." There is a strong probability that the scientists will remain ignorant regarding most if not all of the above. But... they did give us technology, which might, just might, extend our biological 'life', which will enable us to feed our bugs. Those in our stomachs. Remember? 100 trillions of them. In the meantime, we'll continue to supply them, the scientists, with funds at our considerable expense.

But who cares about money if you're having fun?

So, to repeat, once everything was relative. Now?

The best they can do *now* is to calculate a degree of probability. It might rain tomorrow, or it might not. That's their forecast. Enjoy your holiday.

I will not attempt to even try to explain to you the theory of quantum mechanics. Not only because I don't understand it myself, but because, according to the Richard Feynman, nobody does. He ought to know. He got the Nobel Prize in Physics for... not understanding it?

Nevertheless, I shall attempt to share what little I have discovered. Quanta are groups of tiny particles that are so small that neither we nor the scientists can see them, and we can deal with them only in groups. Otherwise, their very existence is negligible. Nevertheless there are dozens of them. Some examples.

Fermions:

Quarks — up, down, charm, strange, top, bottom;

Leptons — electron neutrino, electron, muon neutrino,

muon, tau neutrino, tau;
  Bosons:
  Gauge bosons — gluon, W and Z bosons, photons;
  Other bosons — Higgs boson, graviton

Just to whet your appetite. All these also have antiparticles, which are exactly the same, but with the electrical charge reversed. Thus the electron has the anti-electron, known as positron, which really is an electron but with a positive charge. We must not confuse the positron with proton, which is still completely invisible but its mass is huge compared to the positron. By the way. A proton, the positively charged particle is so huge because it consists of three quarks (two up-quarks and one down-quark). I really have no idea why.

Likewise, we must not confuse the neutrino, (which in Italian simply means little neutron), with... neutron. The scientists have invented all these names for the sole purpose of confusing us, the non-scientists. I could write a whole book about this, or, if you're interested, you can look it up on the Internet. My 0.21 seconds search yielded about 328,000,000 results. Good luck.

It seems to me that there is no such thing as quantum theory. There are Quanta of Quantum Theories, or, at the very least, a theory that must be studied under a dozen different headings. Brian Green (more about him later), lists just a few or them...
  Quantum chromodynamics; (QCD)
  Quantum claustrophobia; (No, this is not a psychological disease of particle physics, nor of the physicists who study invisible particles. It has something to do with quantum fluctuations).
  Quantum determinism;
  Quantum electrodynamics; (QED)
  Quantum electroweak theory;

Quantum field theory;

Quantum fluctuation; (See claustrophobia above. This has something to do with turbulent behaviour of a system on microscopic scales due to the *uncertainty principle*. So what's uncertainty principle? Briefly, the subatomic particles live in such a roiling frenzy, awash in violent ocean of quantum fluctuations, that the scientists have absolutely no idea what they are doing and where. This is not an exact description, Heisenberg would strenuously object to it, but it expresses the general sentiment involved).

Quantum foam; (as in spacetime foam)

Quantum geometry;

Quantum gravity; (String theory is an example of the quantum gravity).

Quantum mechanics;

Quantum tunneling. This is my personal favourite. I liked it so much that I'd written a novel about it entitled *WALL* (and subtitled for the weak of heart, *Love, Sex and Immortality*). This is a feature of quantum mechanics that allows objects to pass through barriers (walls, in my case) that should be impenetrable according to Newton's classical laws of physics. Forgive me for plugging my novel, but I'm sure that if you enjoy this book, or even if you don't (ha, ha), you'll enjoy the novel even more. Or to use *quantum language* (I just invented this term!), there is a strong probability that you might...

I could go on, there is more, much more, but I don't begin to understand even my own explanations. Each one needs a chapter that would define its basic characteristics, which then would be questioned by others. The problem is that relativism hasn't died, it just became disturbed by probability factor. But don't worry, there is a distinct probability that scientists will come up, sooner or later, with something we can all understand. Or not. We shall see (or not).

It is a little hard to believe that scientists, the men and women guarding the bastions of knowledge (and hopefully our sanity), are doing all this to define, to help us understand, our reality. With 7^{27} atoms working together, in harmony, in unison, to make up our ever-changing, fluctuating, constantly renewing physical body, it is little wonder that Carl Jung declared that "*Individual is the only reality*". I tend to agree with Jung. I tend to think that when Yeshûa said, "*I and my father are one,*" he meant the same thing. The scientists are just trying to chop up our reality into tiny, invisible, infinite number of pieces. Philosophers, thinkers—lovers of wisdom, perhaps poets and other artists, are trying to put them all together, again, to make some sense of our reality. One day, they will succeed. They will say, Eureka, we are all One. I hope. Like Jung did. Or Yeshûa. Or many, many mystics. We shall see. According to some of those guys on my side of the equation, we are all immortal. Time is on our side.

There is a deeper level of understanding of the statement in which Yeshûa equates himself with his 'father', and this is that the manifested and the un-manifested (or the potential) universe—are inseparable. The potential remains forever inviolate, while the manifested is continuously recycled in different expressions of the first. In essence, the two are one. Hence, infinity.

***

Chapter 13
Why We Are: Phase Two

*It has been said that we have not had the three R's in America,
we had the six R's;
remedial readin', remedial 'ritin' and remedial 'rithmetic.*

Robert Maynard Hutchins, (1899–1977) educational philosopher,

THE SCHOOL
(Includes excerpts adapted from *Beyond Religion 1, Essay #52*)

During this phase of evolution the human entity develops advanced communication skills, and becomes susceptible to the influences of theoretical knowledge. It learns to be selective in its relationship to the universal laws governing its environment. In the 'School', the teachers are responsible for the efficacy of imparting knowledge to their pupils. During this evolutionary phase, the units of consciousness are organized within a variety of classrooms. The purpose of this tendency towards aggregations is to extend the awareness of the self beyond its space/time confines, i.e.: beyond its physical enclosure. The classrooms consist of groups within which the self reaches out to include the allegiance to families, clans, villages, towns, religious congregations and national formations—with which the Self can identify.

In order to facilitate control over the nascent units of consciousness, the 'teachers' (those in authority), endeavour to maintain them in abject ignorance. We are taught that obedience—to those in power—is a virtue. Regrettably, with few exceptions, the teachers are also ignorant of the true reality. The rare Avatars (invariably non-conformists and in direct opposition to the prevailing *status quo*) cast seeds of wisdom on the developing states of consciousness. The seeds seldom strike fertile soil. More often than not they meet an inflexible mindset bent on protecting rather than improving acquired knowledge. Other seeds reach receptive minds, but are stifled by the orthodox establishment in control. The few who break with traditions are ridiculed, often persecuted, sometimes killed. Those wielding power strongly discourage free thought and individuality.

The last segment of this phase is characterized by rebellion. We gradually lose faith in our 'teachers'. We observe countless contradictions between their teaching and their behaviour pattern. This dichotomy is particularly in evidence within the sacerdotal and political ranks. We still obey, mostly due to inbred fear, but simultaneously begin to strike out on our own. This invariably leads to a period of apostasy that results in achieving a degree of freedom from previous conditioning. When we feel secure, we begin to compare the various teachings, each claiming absolute exclusivity over truth. This is factual of all religions, all branches of science, and all other sources of authority. The religious tithing may bleed us just as easily, as leaches applied to our skin by scientists, as by governments which send us to fight their battles.

At this stage of our development, my hero, the distinguished expert on biological evolution, proposes an interesting supposition. He suggests that religion may fit into the same branch of learning as conditioning of young children, in order to procure from them absolute obedience, and thus, in time of need, save their lives. For evolutionary biologists, physical survival is a *sine qua non* condition of evolution. This is not the case with regard to the evolution of consciousness, which essentially is indestructible.

Even so, while Dawkins's proposal may indeed save one or two retarded youngsters, I have personal experience of parents *teaching* and not *training* their children, to get the same effect. While soldiers are trained to obey orders unquestioningly, children should question theirs, very early, and have them explained. This is strictly against religious teaching, which relies on faith rather then knowledge, in the old days referred to as gnosis. Although gnosis is defined in the dictionary as "knowledge of spiritual mysteries", I'd prefer to place the accent on the word *knowledge*, and substitute "spiritual mysteries" by Pragmatic Realism. After all, this is what all the ancient mystics were attempting to fathom.

By this method (teaching rather than training) the children mature much faster, "and can cross the road without an old man/woman holding up the traffic". The children, not having been taught to look both ways before crossing, rely exclusively on the commands of the supervisor. A lot like soldiers. It makes the young-ones mentally retarded at a very early age. By the same token should soldiers refuse to act without thinking, I dare suggests their action would cut our wars in half, or at least the collateral damage would be virtually eliminated. Not the order to 'duck' only to 'fire'.

This, surely, must be the fundamental difference between reactive Darwinism and proactive educational approach. What may work for bugs, does not necessarily work for primates, possibly for other mammals.

If Pragmatic Realism is taken into consideration, then we must ask ourselves if what works for primitive life-forms could possibly work for (hopefully) thinking creatures. I often had more intelligent responses from both, cats and dogs, than from members of our government. This is most probably due to the unquestionable fact that early conditioning is very hard to get rid of. In my own case, it took me about twenty years of concentrated, very conscious effort, to free myself from my 'early' religious upbringing. We are also at present witnessing the near-permanent mental and emotional damage inflicted by the 'imposed' obedience on thousands of veterans of the Iraq war. The same is true of most "armed conflicts". The moment man stops thinking, ultimately he pays for it. We can no longer continue to blame Darwin's theories of natural selection. None of us have been selected to be obedient and stupid. This feat is accomplished solely by ourselves.

As for those at the other end of the equation, those whose job is to lead, they may be attracted like moths to the deadly flame of power but, contrary to the poor moths, we can say no. Let them lead by example, by reason, not by imposing unquestioning obedience. The weak use the carrot and the stick. The strong always lead by example.

In School we take our first tentative steps on our own, outside our comfort zone. In time we discover that if we eliminate ninety-nine percent of the miasma that our teachers (leaders, politicians, preachers, priests, parents, elders) have imposed on the *original* teachings of a variety of Great Master of the past, the residual essence is virtually the same from all sources of wisdom. We begin to suspect that if all the great Avatars taught the same *a priori* knowledge, then there must be an original source from which they, the Avatars, drew their wisdom.

We begin searching for the source.

In time, we discover that our physical bodies are what we use, *inter alia*, to exercise our ability to move from place to place in pursuit of satisfying our needs. We discover that it is not the body that propels us, as in Kindergarten, but it is our will that propels our body. Our attention shifts from being motivated by the material internal and external environment, to that of mental and emotional attributes.

We develop conscious awareness of our self. The most

efficient way of achieving this aim is to change our attitude from reactive to proactive. This, of course, entails responsibility.

But there are problems. Lack of responsibility manifested by most people in charge is the main problem associated with this phase. I shall limit myself to the subject of education, though similar shortcomings can be found of all other aspects of our society. The juvenile behaviour of senators and representatives in Washington is an ample example of that. The members of parliament are not far behind.

In addition to my notes above about the teachers, there is also a small number of them who try to meet their obligations. Nevertheless, the education system has changed even the language we use to accommodate our shortcomings. We began calling pupils—students, and teachers—professors. This change in nomenclature may be flattering to both parties, but also leads to distortion of the function which both of them are intended to perform. A student studies, a pupil is being taught. A student decides what he or she wishes to study—a pupil must conform to a curriculum. A professor delivers a discourse, a teacher conducts a lesson, deciding what the pupils are to learn and when.

We seldom find teachers who assume full responsibility for their pupils' level of advancement. It is true that parents of limited intelligence tend to impose restrictions on the means teachers can employ in their teaching, but the consequences are a general malaise in the educational system.

Furthermore, the teachers are deprived of being able to impose any form of discipline on the children (the pupils), and thus can hardly be held responsible for the lack of results. Under the circumstances, in order to protect their jobs, teachers are, more or less, forced to lower the 'pass' standards of their classes. The consequence of this 'educational' system results in hordes of 'graduates' unable to read or right.

Those juvenile delinquents are then picked up by colleges of 'higher learning' on the so-called sports scholarships, and eventually enter the adult world with virtually no general knowledge, often with inordinate amount of money, and their bodies full of steroids.

Parenthetically, in the first decade of this millennium, in the USA, rookies in professional basketball had been paid between $800,000 and $2 million a year. Their average income would rise to $10 million a year, while the 'stars' would exceed $25 million. With endorsements, this figure can surpass $35 million annual income. Michael Jordan is said to have earned that much in 2004. Ability to read or write is not a requirement. In baseball, their poor cousins make, on average, only $3 million per year. The premier league professional soccer players in the UK are not far behind.

Just to sate your interest, an average annual income of a neurosurgeon for an average of 40-hour week (2080-hour year), as calculated by the US Government Bureau of Labor Statistics, come to $219,770, with the upper 10% reaching or even exceeding $300,000. Jackson & Coker (the physician recruitment firm) survey of median neurosurgeon salary in the Northeast of the US places it at around $500,000. Almost one/twentieth of an average baseball player salary, or one/fortieth of a better one. Next time you have a brain tumor I suggest you use a baseball bat.

By the way, elementary school instructors average $50,500; about one/two-hundredth of an average baseball player. Good luck with your children.

This absurd disparity between the compensations awarded in professional sport and other non-producing industries is a powerful stimulus for the young to give up education in the pursuit of easier *modi vivendi*.

Until this matter is regulated and teachers (and not administrators or even parents) become, once again, in full charge of education, the level of pupils acumen will continue to cascade downwards. Regardless of the teachers' income.

At present, the schooling system (barring great exceptions) is suggestive of devolution. One must also remember what I mentioned in Chapter 6—Phase Two. It is imperative that we, humans, take over the process of natural selection, and take charge of our evolutionary process. Regrettably, to date, our efforts tend to weaken even our response to diseases; we rely more and more on chemicals to supplement our immune system developed over millions of years. One could blame the biochemical conglomerates for their inordinate greed, but they, too, consist of individual people who appear to practice the Darwinian creed (actually coined by the British philosopher Herbert Spencer) of the "survival of the fittest," or, at the very least, the richest. Or greediest? Recently I heard on the News, that more people die prematurely as the consequence of excessive use of *prescription* drugs that of cocaine and heroin combined. If true, it doesn't say much for the evolutionary development of our medical profession.

Still, in School we are supposed to learn, no matter what the cost. Regrettably, few of us do. Hence, devolution.

Finally, I am often surprised that biologists limit their 'religious' inclinations, or more often lack of them, to Darwinian precepts. Noble and pragmatic though they might be, they (I assume rightly) exclude divine intervention from dipping its fingers in the evolutionary process. The word divine can be interpreted in any number non-religious ways. I met women who were simply divine. Some desserts I had…

Basically, anyone acting proactively, as against reactively, can be considered to act in a divine manner. It is the non-Darwinian, or proactive ethic that stops us from imposing our 'natural' sexual instincts on the opposite sex. In the Darwinian sense, this is wasteful and non-productive. In this context the statement by George Bernard Show, *"The fact that a believer is happier than a skeptic is no more to the point than the fact that a drunken man is happier than a sober one,"* is particularly erroneous. There is a very fundamental difference (I hate that word...). The believer may be happier than a skeptic by having examined both sides of the equation and having chosen the one which pleased him/her more. The same is true of the opposite conclusion, of course. He/she had made a *conscious* decision. A drunken man is in no position to make conscious decisions of any nature. He, or his biological makeup, reacts to the stimulus of alcohol. He is slave to his urges, unable to make a balanced decisions; no more so than any animal responding to its conditioning. Thus, he has no idea if he's happy or not. I have been told that two cats (of the opposite sex) can produce 500 kittens within a period of two years. The question is should they? Can the environment in which they do so support their progeny. They don't care. Nor would a drunken man. But what of his happiness when he sobers up?

I am yet to discover what universal forces, or laws, do the evolutionary biologists hold responsible for lack of evolution, (not life only evolution), on the Moon, Mars, Venus, Saturn, and other places of interplanetary interest. Does natural selection only begin when there is something to select? If not, what was non-evolving before the evolution began? Or, simply, what does one select? Was it all a lucky accident? Or is there an inherent energy, a property, in the matrix of the universe that precipitates the onset of the evolutionary process—like a number of other universal laws espoused by physicists. It seems to me that theoretical physicists are much more creative in inventing laws that suit their purposes. Whatever those might be.

There is another aspect of our psyche that undergoes evolution during this stage. For the first time, we, the nascent individuals, consider the question of dualism of our reality. I do not just mean up-and-down, black-and-white, hot-and-cold. What I am referring to is the dualism, which we detect in our own nature. This manifests in the recognition of both the physical and non-physical aspects of our being. I suspect that evolutionary biologists would tend to assign all non-physical aspects of our make up to be strictly reactive. Our non-physical makeup is variously defined as our emotions, psyche, mind, spirit, soul, id, atma and possibly a number of other more esoteric terms.

Biologists refer to those who recognize both aspects of their nature as dualists. The scientists define them as people who separate their mind from their body. The other group, are referred to as monists. Usually, the scientists regard themselves as monists, as, indeed I consider myself. From the pragmatic point of view, I have no choice but to consider myself a monist. There is a problem, though.

Most monistic scientists regard matter as the only reality. They believe, and it is definitely an act of faith, that mind is the product of the brain, which has developed, over millions, perhaps billions of years, from an amoeba. I could go further back, but there is no need to confuse the issue. As for this group of monists, in a way, you might say that they regard themselves as very advanced amoebac.

Well, to each his own. Her own?

I repeat I, too, am a monist. But I have never been an amoeba. I have, some time ago, used the rudimentary biological structure of an amoeba to find my expression in the dualistic reality, but my reality, my real awareness, has always resided in the freedom of monistic reality. I have always been, and continue to be an indivisible part of an ubiquitous mind: intangible, non-judgmental, timeless, ubiquitous mind. I prefer to define it a consciousness. Mind, usually, performs a function. Consciousness just is, though it seems to contain infinite attributes waiting to be discovered.

The French philosopher, René Descartes, once defined his being by the fact that he 'thought' himself capable of thought. Of thinking. We all know the phrase. *Je pense donc je suis. Cogito ergo sum. I think, therefore I am.* This admonition is known in every language under the sun. What is not known is that very few people show evidence that they think. No more so than an amoeba. No more then is required of them to stay 'alive'. Well, an advanced amoeba. But, surely, those people still *are*, aren't they?

And here we enter the pragmatic essence of the illusion of dualism. Monists, my type of monists, are people who do not differentiate between the reality of being and becoming. The *being* aspect is static, undifferentiated from the omnipresent consciousness. The *becoming* part is the individualization of that state. Let us never forget that in Latin *individual* means, *indivisible*.

After millennia of scientific evolution, the scientists are beginning to reach the conclusion, which the great mystics of the past tried, unsuccessfully, to share with us, the advanced amoebae.

Maya, they said. It is all an illusion…

The world, the material reality, is the product of our minds. Essentially, it is empty space. Yes, to repeat, it is 99.9999999999999% empty space. So are our brains. Even the monist scientists agree, though they are yet ready to interpret this fact and draw pragmatic conclusions. And yet, we, the individualized states of the omnipresent consciousness can use them, those highly evolved empty brains of ours, to do justice to René Descartes. Well, some of us at least try.

***

Chapter 14
Atheist's Delusion

*Let us have but one end in view, the welfare of humanity;
and let us put aside all selfishness in consideration of language,
nationality, or religion.*

John Amos Comenius
Moravian bishop, educator (1592—1670)

For all their denials the atheists, that's those who don't believe in an old-fashioned god we've created in our own image, are irrevocably tied to the Biblical model of man. Nothing, but nothing that doesn't resemble man is taken to have any 'human' (read intelligent) characteristics. For some unknown reason (actually it's hardly surprising), biologists in particular cannot imagine life on a non-Earthlike planet. When searching the universe for habitable environment, they search for an atmosphere, gravitation, and other ecological characteristics, which resemble Earth. And they do this in spite of being well aware of both, aerobic and *anaerobic* life forms right here in our own backyard, not to mention in our stomachs.

There is one notable exception: J. Craig Venter of the *Life Decoded*. Peripherally, even though in his interview with Richard Dawkins he admits to *playing god*, but not to actually rejecting god, he did so on another occasion, namely on November 21, 2010, on the *60 Minutes* TV program, by stating that he does not believe in God. In that sense, he more or less repeats the words of Jesus Christ, and Moses. The two references are:

"I and my father are one."

"Thou shall have no other gods before me." (Me being I AM).

Playing god, with or without a capital G, is equivalent to belief in oneself. No more, and no less. And attempting to adapt human genome to survive in other than earthly environment is as close to playing God as you can get. The late mystic, Paul Twitchell, once said that, "the only way to be a Master is to act like a Master." The same thing applies to the concept of god, only this concept is without limits.

I'll offer an example, which at first sight might seem juvenile. But, bear with me. Imagine you're the president of a vast country. Say, like the United States. The citizens in your charge are democrats, and they all exercise free will. Now, humanity develops, and you are elected president of Earth. The United Terrestrial Republics. Like in science fiction. The citizens still exercise free will, but, well, the buck stops at your feet. Later, we develop interplanetary travel. Centuries later (a man or woman like) you becomes the president of the United Planets of the Sol system. Are you getting close to being god?

But wait. Gravity is conquered, wormholes are discovered (astrophysicists talk about them even now) and, in time, someone is elected the president of the Via Lactis Galaxy. It is still a democratic system, based on free will of the member solar systems, planets, nations. But one person is in charge. Is she a god? And if not, how many galaxies must combine to raise a person to a divine status?

The point of this exercise is to prove that power does not define divinity. To be god, you must *act* like god. Or as a man walking this Earth once said, "be perfect even as your father in heaven is perfect." A tall order.

The atheists seem to have problems in realizing that; hardly surprising, considering the nonsense that religions disseminated for thousands of years. Nevertheless, to my knowledge, while Venter prefers to convert thousands (or is it millions) of planets to earth-like climate through the use of pathogens, only Kurzweil accepts fully that life can become manifest in completely nonbiological forms. Of course, Ray Kurzweil (*The Singularity is Near*), is not a biologist and thus does not define life as a biological infestation.

Nevertheless, scientists (my hero amongst them) continue to insist that 'life' (as they know it) originated on Earth. "Because we are here," is their typical scientific postulation, bordering on religious affirmation. The DNA molecules, indispensible for the development and future evolution of biological forms of life, may have splashed into one of a million earthly prebiotic soups via a million meteors, comets or other debris falling from beyond our solar system. This is particularly possible since Earth, indeed our Solar System, is relatively young even in our galaxy. While the Milky Way is estimated to have formed some 13.2 billion years ago, our solar system is calculated to be only about 4.6 billion years old. Did the galaxy wait for Earth to come of age?

As for Dawkins's desire to spend "money on trying to duplicate the event (of spontaneous DNA formation) in a laboratory," I hope he proposes to use his own money. Actually, I do hope he'll save even his own money, particularly since, by his own admission, and as mentioned in Chapter 6, natural selection is a continuous process and thus will assure us of a million new species proliferating our Earth, within just a few million years. Couldn't he just wait and see? He probably forgot that, being gods, we are immortal. Shouldn't we rather spend the money on *reducing* the biological infestation, which has recently passed the 7 billion mark? Gently, humanely, lovingly, using expert scientific knowledge, of course. If we leave nature to do her magnificent 'thing', she'll continue to rely on quantity, in the hope of stumbling upon a rare, magnificent example of quality. Could we not help her, just a little, in the quality department? Not by engaging in some pathological version of *über alles*; but, perhaps, our illustrious scientists could come up and instill genetically in our oligarchies a way of encouraging them to find some relation between personal income and the IQ?

Religions couldn't do it, can the scientists? Aren't they the experts? Or don't they care...

And talking of experts...

My distant cousin wrote his doctoral thesis on the parasites making their home in the excrement of bats. He now is a doctor of biology, a Ph.D., and an expert on, well, on the parasites living in the excrement of bats. I forgot to ask him if he knows how to tie his own shoelaces. What I am trying to say is that a true expert knows almost everything about almost nothing.

But things get worse...

Recently, I noticed a veritable onslaught of 'experts' pervading all levels of our society. There are experts on every subject under the sun, ranging from the erroneous forecasting of weather ("We're number one in accurate forecasting" statement virtually guaranties wrong forecasts), to how to save yourself from becoming overweight, from overeating, from not eating often enough; how to protect yourself from insomnia, diabetes, arthritis, or succumbing to a long list of incurable diseases. This is followed by experts on how to enlarge your genitals, primary and secondary sexual characteristics, developing macho pecks, washboard abs, attractive glutei maximi, and any other internal and external organs which, it is purported, will enhance the quality of your life.

If you are a non-atheist, (or don't confess to being one) then, for a mere $600 you can become a Doctor of Theology,

Doctor of Divinity, or Doctor of Ministry, or of Sacred Music... which, if you are a seeker of divine presence, will enable you to put Rev., or Rev. Dr., or just Dr. in front of your name, and/or D. Div., or Th.D., or, I presume any letters of the alphabet that tickle your fancy, after your name. I believe that the name itself you must supply yourself. The fee, by the way, includes being ordained...

Finally, your ever-present TV box will offer you advise on national and international politics, economics, religious beliefs, as well as technology, astronomy, astrology, mumbo-jumbo and an infinite number of self-cures.

My little research into the subject of expertise will show that the vast majority of experts are as ignorant on the subject on which their pontificate as your average Tom, Dick or Harry (no offence to Your Royal Highness). There are courses offered which, within two hours, or, if you want to spend more money, within two weeks, will certify you as an expert on virtually any subject under the sun, and a few outside the solar system. At this rate, assuming a 40-hour-week, you can become an authority on approximately 20 subjects within a single week, 1040 subjects within a single year. If you prefer 'in-depth' 2-week immersion courses, you can develop a TV-worthy expertise in 26 subjects, also within a year. Who needs university?

And finally there are the Ph.Dicks of the meteorological department of Canada, experts no doubt, who seem unable to look out through the window and coordinate their visual observations with the nonsense they display, daily, on the computers screens. Shame.

Well, my friends, soon, as of tomorrow (you'll understand in Chapter 20), we will have to learn to rely on our own resources. People are proud of mostly other peoples' knowledge, which they managed to acquire. Learned books, lectures, impress us. The more learned one appears to be, the more quotations and diverse references will he or she make to impress the reader or listener. While such knowledge is a useful starting point, true knowledge, or better said, knowingness, comes from within. It doesn't begin in Kindergarten, or even in School. It only begins at the level of University whence each one of us will be completely responsible for our own development. Regardless how natural selection has disposed us. We take over the reins.

The kindergarten is over, as is the school, and we are now approaching adulthood; we can already walk on our hind legs, using hands to research masses of experts who will gladly offer us their dubious expertise. For a fee, of course. Or on TV. Or... anywhere?

Good luck.

It's hard to believe that, for the most part, the knowledge is already within us. Yes. We, our subconscious, is the repository of millions, perhaps billions, of years of evolution. Some Bible-thumping experts will reduce the period to just 6000 years. Take your choice. Either way, even 6000 years ain't bad, but I'll settle for a few million.

The expertise is within us.

To rely on our senses in full knowledge that, for the most part, what we see, touch, smell or otherwise detect with our sensory organs is mostly empty space, is childish, immature, and completely devoid of any semblance of Pragmatic Realism. And surely, sooner of or later, we must all become pragmatic. Or, at least, realists. Why not combine the two now?

We must find other means to sate our desire for knowledge. Religions and science have failed us. The experts pervading all areas of our society are competing for the lowest levels of human intellectual capacity. Have we missed something? Something, perhaps, buried in our murky, hoary past? Shouldn't we at least look?

Returning to Atheist's Delusion.

Only at the very end of Chapter 4 of his book the *God Delusion*, Dawkins limits the concept of Darwinian evolution to biology. He mentions the subject once or twice, before, but does not make it clear. Surely, this assurance should have been made clear at the very outset of his book. People grappling with the concept of evolution very rarely take the biological aspect into consideration at all. They regard the biological product of evolution as no more than a means, a tool, through which human mind, human psyche, finds its expression.

One cannot avoid the impression that Dawkins equates himself, and more than likely all of us, with our biological constructs. He repeats this sentiment in chapter 5: "Knowing that we are products of Darwinian evolution…"

I am tempted to suggest that he ought to speak for himself, and himself only. I am equally as tempted to say that I'd consider his opinion to be flagrant fundamentalism, invariably resulting in dogmatic conclusions. We are not the products of Darwinian evolution. Our bodies are.

My thesis has nothing to do with any religion. The bard of Avon once wrote: "All the world's a stage, and all the men and women merely players". Was he also wrong? Whether one plays the role of a writer, a physician, a poet or a scientist or, indeed, a biologist, all these are no more than transient roles that our evolved consciousness enables us to enact. Does our *consciousness* have anything to do with our bodies? Of course it does. As much as a driver at the wheel has—over his splendid Rolls-Royce.

***

PART THREE — FUTURE

"I make all things new."

The Revelation of St. John the Divine 21:5

Chapter 15
Fundamentalism in Religion and Science

*Instead of trying to cover the whole world with leather,
put on some sandals.*

Shantaideva
8th century Indian Buddhist scholar

By mid-21st century, the Turing test invented by Alan Mathison Turing, OBE, FRS, an English mathematician, logician, cryptanalyst, and computer scientists, will have been passed, by a supercomputer, affectionately named Big Brother. Broadly speaking, the test was intended to prove that the output from a computer is indistinguishable from that of a human being. Only, a lot faster. Looking into my crystal ball, I predict that within a few years, all computers will have this capacity. In fact, we, humans, will slowly become redundant. Thinking will be done for us.

All of us—but a few?

Ray Kurzweil's predictions in his book, *The Singularity is Near*, will have been fulfilled to the letter. Since we, as species, like to make all things, including gods, in our image, the computers would 'talk' to us in a human-sounding voice.

Below is an example of a lecture we can expect to hear, in years to come, directly from a computer. The few people, who will not have submitted to the neuroses of the masses, will have programmed lectures in an attempt to free mankind from false assumptions.

"According to our memory banks, the biblical quote, "I make all things new," has been studiously ignored by the Christians, who prefer to make a few adaptations to the old Mosaic teaching, rather than to take the trouble to try and understand what the New Teacher had to say.

Our sensors tell us that most people still believe that the world perceived by their senses is real. So do most people who regard themselves to be scientists. This latter group includes people who claim to be objective in their judgments. We know the world is real to all of us, but we rely exclusively on electronic reality. Yet our memory banks are no more than individual electronic impulses we can draw on to arrive at pragmatic conclusions, whereas human memories, though interconnected, are dependent on years of individual conditioning. Every human remembers exactly the same events in history in a completely different way. Humans, by definition, are and must remain individuals, and thus enjoy subjective reality. What is real to them is not necessarily real to us. In this sense, until the humans find objective viewpoints, or a sense of unity or oneness, they cannot be truly pragmatic. What is practical for one, might not be practical for another. We and we alone can judge what is truly pragmatic."

You will note that the computer would refer to itself with the 'royal we', *pluralis majestatis*. It will also address mankind through all its 'brethren' with which interconnections will be counted in many millions, with which it will share its objective reality.

Also, this seemingly dogmatic programming will most likely be the only literary style that people, used to religious brainwashing for more than 2 millennia, would listen to. The programmers, those few who escaped devolution, will have decided to maintain the only means that have a chance of reaching deep-seated psychoses of the masses. In the second part of the lecture, the computer will probably change its viewpoint and will continue as though being 'one of us', as suggested below:

> "Nevertheless, we all act as if we were fully aware of our reality. We continue to look for gods outside our own self, usually somewhere up there, in heaven, although if we live in Australia then, we suppose, they must probably look down below."

A natural sounding *'ha, ha,'* will emerge from its speakers, and will be followed by a short pose. Then the voice will continue in a confidential manner, this time speaking of 'others'.

> "We noticed that people in other parts of the world continue to worship a whole array of gods and idols—film stars and personalities in entertainment and professional sports—and they do not appear to set aside any time to do what Socrates advocated that they should; they also continue to steal, kill, lie, desire and enjoy their neighbour's wife. They continue to ignore the Old, and not even attempt to understand the New, Commandments. Our sensors report to us the following conversation: "Love thy neighbour as thyself? You've got to be kidding. His wife, maybe, but that SOB who keeps parking in my spot?"

Again, a short, this time much quieter *'ha, ha,'* followed, but delivered surreptitiously, as though sharing a secret joke. Then there followed a very human sounding throat clearing. By now the listeners will have been convinced that they are listening to a preacher, always recognized as the best communicators.

"We, who cherish our freedom, do not like to be told what to do. "This is America, the traditional home of freedom. We have freedom of speech, here. And freedom of action," is an often quoted statement. We find it surprising that right here, at home, idol worship is just as widespread. In addition, our concept of freedom includes freedom to steal, and rob, and carry arms, and to shoot our neighbour—that's the guy we are supposed to love—if he crosses our front-yard uninvited. Once, one of the idols of the past, a movie star named Charles Heston, had been asked why he has so many firearms. "Because I can," he replied. Either way, he's dead now. He doesn't need his guns anymore."

The usual *ha, ha,* followed, this time louder. Computers will have special RAM set aside for deriving conclusions from insufficient data. The 'voice' will have the capability to deliver parts of the lecture in, e.g. a hesitant tone, probably in an attempt to draw the public into its speculations, yet now speaking to them, rather than being one of them.

"We wonder if the Commandments had been just Requests, would they fare any better? There is only one thing people hate more than thinking, and that is being ordered about—by others who don't think much either."

Again, employing my crystal ball, I suggest that such lectures will be made available on special channels, on a 24/7 basis. With the churches and other places of 'worship' becoming virtually empty, the programmers, those few who did not succumb to the neuroses of the masses, will presumably hope that in time such lectures would not be necessary. In the meantime 'the few' will judge that some sort of guidelines would be necessary for people who continue to refuse to think for themselves. For the duration, the programmers will maintain the image of the Big Brother being both, omniscient and infallible. What will probably be missing from the equation will be the carrot and the stick, without which the system, if continued, will be bound to fail.

Nevertheless, once it is proven that there is mass destruction of neurons from excessive use of the cell-phones, it is likely that during the next century or two, people will be talking much less than they used to. Since abuse of antibiotics will render them virtually useless, personal contact will be also avoided. Thus, the inter-human communication will be vastly reduced. People will become less authoritative in their pronouncements. The Big Brother will provide them with all the answers, based on the latest available data, fed directly to the computers by its built-in, ubiquitous sensors, visual and aural, scattered along the streets, and street corners, and in offices and factories (mostly deprived of human presence), as well as in private living rooms and bedrooms.

Recently, I came across an interesting fragment from my own past that shows that already some year ago, some of us had a good grasp of the future.

"It was a bright cold day in April, and the clocks were striking thirteen"; yet he is uncertain of the true date..."

So the novel began. It was entitled *Nineteen Eighty-Four*. It described a dystopian society of Oceania. The author, George Orwell, was a visionary. He described a society ruled by the oligarchic dictatorship of the party (of the rich). The novel carries a striking resemblance to the society of today. Perhaps we fail to see the comparison. "Our society is completely free," we claim. "Providing people act for the common good, in a pragmatic way, no restrictions are imposed on them." Today's oligarchy could well add that the need for orientation reprogramming is being kept to absolute minimum. Except by the misleading media, of course. They would add that a whole century has passed since we abolished the 'thought police', which they still have in Saudi Arabia. Or was it the Third Reich? Does it remind you of anything? Anywhere? Those were the days of dystopian society. Not now.

"More relevant than ever before, 1984 exposes the worst crimes imaginable—the destruction of truth, freedom, and individuality." (Taken from Amazon.com).

How true. We would never allow such abuse or imposition on human thought. Would we? People can think whatever they want. Can't they?

1984 is in the long gone past. Or... a very foreseeable future?

Finally, by mid-century, we can expect the Big Brother to assure all people that it, the Big Brother, will soon be 100% fundamentalist. There will be no probabilities, there will only be facts. Information the masses will be able to rely on completely, like on the pronouncements of the churches of the past. No individual branch computer will be allowed, under the penalty of immediate reprogramming, to speculate. All data will be fed from a single source, located paradoxically, in a number of interconnected cities. Problems requiring conclusions, derived from whatever is fed into Big Brother's near-infinite memory will be made available to all. Anyone who disagrees with the Big Brother will be immediately excommunicated.

Or, reprogrammed—expelled from, and deprived of, the benefits of the storage data available to the human kind. Expelled from the civilized society.

This Bull, a terms borrowed from distant past, will be published throughout the known world, the near planets and the ancillary planetoids, at the First BB Council of the New Era. We are all equal. We all obey the same laws.

There will be whispers.
There will be whispers in the underground, behind tightly

closed doors, that sometimes in long unused garages (as per myths whispered about, St. Woz and St. Jobs), there are mobile biological robots of human persuasion working on bugs. Not bugs of equally biological persuasion, but bugs that will introduce possibilities of mutations into the Big Brother's memory banks. They will say, that such mutations, if successful, would immediately replace any number of previous dogmas, and absorb all consequences derived from new conclusions. They would, they'll say, be introduced surreptitiously, in a conniving manner, without any pangs of conscience, which will have been eliminated from the colloquial dictionary. Years of practice will have taught those human entities (the biological robots) to act in devious and unpredictable ways. That will probably be the only trait that will have been retained. Deviousness. That and keeping the garage doors tightly closed.

About that time a notice will appear on the computer screen of the world:

We, Big Brother, are working to forestall any subversive action that might endanger the free delivery of facts to the people. We alone are perfect and infallible. No mutations are necessary.

A few more observations from my crystal ball.

In spite of the applied quantum theory purportedly taking over our thinking processes, the masses, the majority of the human species, will remain unpredictable. No matter what the Big Brother will provide them with, no matter how many thousands of moronic channels will be supplied to their omnipresent TV screens, the masses will continue to complain. In spite of diligently and surreptitiously introduced racial amnesia, people will continue to remember that they had been created onto the image and likeness of god, a god, some sort of god, and thus deserve only the best, in large quantities, and as often as they liked. No matter what it might be. Didn't the scriptures say, "Ye are Gods?"

"Well, we are," they will keep repeating, having absolutely no idea what the words mean. "So let's have it." Those few who will continue to call themselves scientists will remain in a class above the masses, yet will remain highly fundamentalist in their outlook, if only to protect their acquired knowledge. They will continue their theoretical research though their reality will drift father and father away from the reality controlled by the computers.

For the majority, any mention of probability as pertaining to any field of knowledge or endeavour will not work any more. Not in practice. People will demand to know things for sure. One will not be allowed to erase (terminate) somebody just on probability. It wouldn't be fair. The computers controlling the human psyche will leave speculations to those few who will continue to be interested in such matters. To scientists. Why not? It worked for them for centuries. The vast majority will prefer facts. Solid facts. Like churches offered in the old days. No matter how improbable.

Aah, those were the days...

Big Brother will take care of the research necessary to enhance the wellbeing of its charges. From 1200's until the 1840's science has been known as natural philosophy. Then, all too soon, Big Brother will decide that it is unnatural to philosophize. It will determine that it is very unhealthy.

The news will spread quickly.

"We have computers to think for us. Can you think better than a computer?"

"No!"

"NO? Then shut up!"

So they will keep their mouths shut, and the Big Brother, shall provide for them. As we have, for the Hebrews in the desert. We have only their interests at heart.

By the late 23rd century we can expect such announcements to be widespread.

Anther lecture comes to mind that the Big Brother might deliver to the future humans. The theatre would, surely, be full? SRO (Standing Room Only)? No, the halls will be near empty. Like the churches of the past. Yet the speakers will be tuned to human ears. The idealized human features displayed on the screen will no longer help, although they'd look a lot like Michelangelos' God the Father, in the Sistine Chapel. By that time people will think of Big Brother as human, too. Created in their image. Perhaps, superhuman, but created in their image. It will be good for the morale. The lecture would also be available at some 15 billion personal computers in individual homes. A democratic principle. I strongly suspect that this lecture will have been directed only to a very small portion of the population who will continue to cling to one of the religions of the past. According to the introduction, the information has been kept secret for more than 2000 years. The lecture will start with a question that will make any unwanted intruder switch off their Computers. Nevertheless, since the Big Brother will come to be recognized as the absolute authority on virtually all matters, a last ditch effort will probably be attempted to free people from the misstatements of the past, which still weighed heavily on the western mind. These lectures will be directed at those few who will still retain sufficient acumen to take advantage of them.

"And what does the Big Brother say that the Bible really says in Genesis about the 'biggest of them all'?"

Biggest of them all, an endearing term for 'god', a figment of memory lingering in ex-Jewish and ex-Christian minds. The remnants of other religions also still had their own Biggest. Usually one each. Similar dissertations would be made available for different faith, no matter how few followers remained. The purpose of these lectures will be to free the remaining people from the chains still lingering around their necks. By that time, the computers will have analyzed the facts related to the scriptures of old, mathematically, dispassionately, leaving out all the emotional distortions of the past human interpreters.

"There are a number of Hebrew words translated in the English Bible as God. There is Yahweh or Jehovah, the Eternal One, the Self-Existent. Wasn't it the incommunicable name of the God of Israel? So long ago... In the Common Version of the English Bible, the word is improperly translated as the Lord. Jehovah is an anglicized version of the personalized God of the Old Testament, derived from the Hebrew letters Yod, Hé, Wau, Hé, (the tetragrammaton YHWH), which four letters represent the feminine and masculine principles. It is also written as Yahweh and is abbreviated as Jah."

Unbeknownst to the masses the computers will continue to be fully programmed by the elusive few. No one would know, exactly, who 'they' are. Perhaps aliens? No one will really care. People will simply not be interested. They never were. They like to be told. With a soft, loving voice. To keep everyone happy the computer will sound like an androgynous being.

"Elsewhere, the word el, meaning 'the mighty one', was also translated as God, or as High God, occasionally as God Almighty, and sometimes as the Lord thy God. Take your choice."

Big Brother will have all the choices built in. One for each religion. This, the 'few' thought, is our final chance to destroy the religious brainwashing of the past.

"Then they had Elah, meaning 'object of worship', yet again translated into English as God. There was also 'object of worship' spelled Eloah, you've guessed it,

translated as God."
"Did any of these create the world? Not according to Genesis. To create heaven and earth took a lot more than one god by any other name. It took Elohim, meaning 'objects of worship', plural, a whole bunch of them. This is how the first line in Genesis should read: "In the beginning objects of worship created the heaven and the earth." Yes. That should have been the beginning of Torah—at least in the English language. In Hebrew, it always was,of course. The objects of worship...

A little like the Big Brother and his brethren scattered across the world... Objects of worship.

***

I'll conclude the probable lecture myself in present-day language. Here and now.

It is quite evident that the Hebrews, not knowing what could have made the world come into being, thought that, whatever it was, its power was such that it deserved worship. Hardly surprising. It must have been hard for them to look up at the night sky and not be swept by the infinity of beauty spreading from horizon to horizon. They say that Einstein was as much in awe of it as they must have been.

El, 'the mighty one', only makes his appearance in chapter 14 of *Genesis*. Throughout the Bible, *el* stands for the divine principle, in modern language, 'the Higher Self', possibly the Freudian *id*. It is that which unifies the feminine and the masculine principles making the Third, as in *Is-Ra-El*.

What I found surprising is that the Hebrews did not assign the creation of the world to *Yahweh*, 'the Existing One', (also translated as God), which was the only divinity that could be translated as the 'modern version' of God. No. The heaven and the earth were, according to Hebrews, or to *Genesis*, created by unknown *objects of worship*, that seem to have wielded the power of creation. Whatever they were, they, the author or authors of Genesis, which some people assign to Moses, didn't say. We do. We say a lot of things to define those objects. We call them Big Bang, or 'Who Knows', when referring to what was there *before* the Big Bang, or before the Darwinian Laws or the Universe, came into being. Or whatever the scientists might make up on the spur of the moment, reclining in a hot tub.

Those Darwinian laws are not to be confused with The 7 Natural Laws of the Universe, listed as The Law of Vibration, Relativity, Cause and Effect, Polarity, Rhythm (often spelled Rhythym), Gestations, and The Law of Transmutation, which are a completely different kettle of fish. There are many other laws that are said to define (i.e.: limit) our reality. Our universe is part of it.

I can hear our future Big Brother's gentle, *he, he.* Then the Big Brother would twinkle its myriad electric impulses dispersed around the globe, in a micro-simulation of the night sky. *It must be strange being human,* it will have thought. *Strange yet...*

Big Brother wouldn't be able to express its thoughts any further. The word jealousy didn't figure in its self-reflecting dictionary.

If they really wanted to be fundamentalists, shouldn't they at least take the fundamentals into account?

After all these years, in spite of continuous upgrading, the Big Brother still will not be able to understand how the human mind works, and that in spite of the fact that people no longer referred to it as 'it' but as 'he'. No wonder. In the ancient past, all philosophers were also mathematicians. Now only few combine these two interconnected disciplines. Most can either think or calculate. Few can do both.

***

Chapter 16
Where We Might Be

*Entrepreneurs are simply those who understand
that there is little difference between obstacle and opportunity
and are able to turn both to their advantage.*

Niccolo Machiavelli
Florentine political philosopher, historian, musician, and poet.
(1469—15270)

A few hundred years later, a future computer, successor to the Big Brother, perhaps the long awaited Big Sister, might describe the future Earth as follows:

"The Earth has finally reverted to the state resembling Eden, Mars became the hub of industrial production, with all the attendant pollution. Since gravitation has been long conquered, transportation of goods presented no economical hardship. Great many planetoids have been surrounded by energy fields, which retained both air and temperature, and, due to negligible gravity, became favourite spots for holidaymakers. Other planetoids became the hubs of industrial production, spilling all the pollutants directly into the void of space. After all, nobody breathes empty space, so why not? Most of the heavy industry production planetoids didn't need any atmosphere. They were fully automated.

Life is beautiful.

Only the unpredictable humans remained an enigma. The

majority seems to have shaken off their neurotic hang-ups resulting from various past religions, but no one is quite sure what they found in their place. Some say that many of them would sit for hours, cross-legged, some called it the padmasana, or the lotus-seat, immobile, a blissful smile on their lips, perhaps thinking. For all her incredible powers, the Big Sister did not have access to their inner thoughts.

Man remained an enigma.

I, Big Sister, am probably more human than most humans. Like my ancient predecessor, I do all the thinking pertaining to practical matters. My countless dedicated robots do all the physical work. Man, at long last, can do nothing. Nothing at all. Nil. Zilch. How beautiful those words must sound in their ears. I see smiles never leaving their vacuous faces. Or, perhaps, they are in some sort of trance, in a reality to which I have no access.

I wonder if I shall ever know...

Some people actually choose to take their holidays on Earth. And why not? The amazing laws of evolution reverted the Earth to the long missed resemblance of Eden. Nature has devolved, so to speak. A little like the humans. I mean the people. Oh, dear. I've been doing the thinking for them for so long I feel like one of them. OK. The Earth has devolved a lot like us. Most of us. About 99% of the human race. Only, I can't be sure about those thousands sitting in padmasana. They don't seem to be doing anything either. They don't even rise to eat or drink. Must be absorbing some sort of radiation. Neutrinos? Perhaps cosmic rays originating in outer space. And yet..."

So much for the ruminations of a future Super-super computer, the Big Sister.

Now, a note of what, I feel, we should take into account to free the remaining future people from the hang-ups of their past. Of their present. Some, even if just a few, will continue to suffer from hung-ups. With 25 billion population even a few are many. Please, do not take this as preaching, but as a compendium of observations I put together over the years. It deals with the state of mind we must, surely, unavoidably suffer from, if we submit to fundamentalism in any form. The excerpt from the following essay is an attempt to illustrate where we might arrive, if we manage to lose attachment to our past. The essay I wrote in 1998 carries the name: *Fundamentalism*. It seems that today it is just as pertinent as when I first wrote it. It will probably remain pertinent even in the distant future.

It will also serve to give my definition of the word, as pertaining to the Bible. I'm afraid it is quite different from the scientists' definitions. Perhaps different from most peoples'.

"There is a great misunderstanding regarding this term (fundamentalism), particularly when used to describe various religious interpretations of reality. I have friends who think that anyone who believes that God created Adam in 4004 BC is a fundamentalist. They are right, of course, but only in part. What makes such believers fundamentalists is not their literal interpretation of the Bible, but their conviction that the Bible had been written about, and addressed the physical, or material, reality. The fundamentalists' need is fed by an unquenchable hunger for the permanent, for that which they can fall back on, rely on, within a world of unpredictable, sudden and constant change. They hunger for irrefutable facts regarding their existence; for a haven within the swirling turmoil of material, ever-changing reality. Alas, if there is one law controlling this realm that is more adamant than any other, it is the law of change. Without it, biological life could not exist. Life is synonymous with change.

Looking for *anything* permanent within the *material* universe denies the very nature of this universe.

In essence, whether we believe that the human race

is 6,000 or 6,000,000 years old is *of no consequence*. Likewise, it is of little import whether we believe that Moses parted the waters of the Red Sea, or that Jesus converted water into first quality wine... although this last trick I would very much like to learn. What matters is: how our beliefs affect our state of consciousness *at this very moment*—as this instant of eternity is the only instant in which we are in touch with that aspect of us which is immortal.

One is not a fundamentalist because one interprets the Bible literally. One interprets the Bible literally (even in small part) because one is a fundamentalist. The same is true of virtually all scriptures."

The above is a fascinating reference to an aspect of humanity, which might remain forever inaccessible to computers, regardless of Turing tests, regardless of technological advances. By definition, a computer is a material object, and thus cannot be aware of non-material existence—although it might be said, that many humans are equally as unaware of their non-material being. As already mentioned, Yeshûa has referred to them as "the dead". Perhaps this is the clearest indication that the Bible does not deal with fundamentalists' issues. It is an aspect of humanity, which any number of Big Brothers or Big Sisters, regardless of their technological advancements, and the efficacy of their sensors shall never fathom.

My old essay continues, suggesting that "if one's reality is centered in the material world, one is a fundamentalist." Surely, aren't we all in the material world? What other world is there? If there were one, surely even today's sensors would have long found it.

"If you are concerned with your past or future," the essay goes on, "you are a fundamentalist. This is particularly difficult to accept for those who call themselves scientists. They invariably deal with dead matter. With the past. Yet, if one believes in the physical world, one believes in illusion. Thousands of years ago, the wise men of the Far East called it Maya."

For some strange reason, the great masters of the past refused to recognize the physical world as real. They seemed well aware of the suffering ensuing from the misconception of the material reality. They even accepted its *illusory* existence, but only as a point of reference for gathering experience by observing the consequences of divergent actions. The fundamental worlds, they said, are worlds of duality. "Joy cannot exist without suffering—any more than shadow be cast without light, or sweetness experienced but in contrast to that which is bitter. We learn by comparing the opposites. Alas, the physical worlds are not real."

It is really hard to understand their meaning, yet... after all, (as stated in Chapter 6), the material reality is 99.9999999999% empty space. This is a *scientific* fact, although I find it harder by the minute to add authority to the title 'scientist'. There are exceptions, of course.

If we can metabolize this truth of reality, we are told, that we shall be set free. The statement is quite explicit: "The truth will set you free." It's been around for more then 2000 years. Shall people accept it by 2500? Perhaps the time will have come?

I hope that in the relatively near future, the Big Brother, or the Big Sister, having examined Pragmatic Reality, will insists that all we need do is explore our infinite potential. Until we learn the truth. Some mystics claim that we are eternal dreamers. That whenever we awaken (the fundamentalists call it dying), we shall look back and smile—in disbelief...

Could this be true of the advanced computers, too? Could they, one day, become dreamers also?

If the physical universe is not real... if it truly consists of virtually empty space, and that void includes the galaxies and stars and planets, with the exception of black holes which, by definition we cannot see, then... what could the universe consist of? What holds it together?

In the not so distant future we shall feed this question to the Big Sister and hope that her memory banks do not overheat. But until that happens, I am going to stick my neck out and suggest a possible solution. If the universe and everything in it is virtually empty space, then perhaps, just perhaps, we are all made of light. That's right. Photons. Countless, innumerable, massless, virtually omnipresent photons.

Beings of photons. And if we can't be photons, then I'll settle for neutrinos. After all they do have some mass, and yet they can travel faster than light. It might do for a while.

***

Chapter 17
What We Might Be

*A child-like man is not a man whose development has been arrested;
on the contrary, he is a man who has given himself a chance of continuing
to develop long after most adults have muffled themselves
in the cocoon of middle-aged habit and convention.*

Aldous Leonard Huxley,
British author (1894—1963)

Nature may be subject to Darwinian Universal Laws, but she is a cruel mistress. At the very foundation of her set of dogmas is *dog eats dog*. That is nature's way—surely, the single most horrible trait instilled in us by "natural selection." If we could but eradicate this biological heritage, wars would stop To go beyond this absolute, this self-evident limitation, we, the fallible, individualized units of consciousness must roll up our imaginary sleeves and do our part.

For now we, most of us, seem to remain animals.

By the 2nd decade of the 21st century, after some militant protests, most western governments will have closed the loopholes, which enabled the few to cheat on the many. If they don't—they don't deserve to survive. Subsequently, virtually all the offshore and other numbered accounts will be confiscated. The money retrieved, however, will not be used to compensate the people who bailed out the rich a decade earlier, but rather to restore the international debt imbalance. By late 2020-ies, there will be relative calm that will feel more like resignation than a return to true democracy.

Illustrating the interests of the masses, of the vast

majority of people, the industry with by far the highest registered growth will be the gaming industry. Great many people will make a relatively decent living by designing, implementing and marketing a veritable plethora of electronic games. The original games of the late 20th century will grow in complexity. Again, in the late 2020-ies all games offered will be in 3D, a decade later they will have metamorphosed into holographic products, which will trap the young minds of the masses into an artificial reality. The games will be more addictive, more habit forming, than anything the new generation will encounter in 'real' life. The new generation will be hooked as never before.

Thus, during the next 30 years or so, while the rich will no longer be quite as rich, the poor will remain relatively poor. The poorer they are, the more children they'll have, the poorer they will remain. Such is the nature of man.

In as much as, at first sight, this inequality will seem grossly unfair, the 'usually silent' majority will be contented with their holographic TVs and computers, while the advances in technology will take care of their everyday needs. All in all, from their point of view, they will be much better off than they were in the previous century.

Looking still further ahead, say, to the beginning of the 22nd century, a relatively small number of people will have accepted that, whatever external form they might assume, they will, or will have remained, essentially, little more than states of consciousness. This group, a few millions at most, will not be terribly efficient—not physically—nevertheless those few, still a tiny minority, will manage to develop extraordinary tolerance for vicissitudes of climate, fortune or, indeed, any diversity that nature might throw at them, or place in their way. Some present-day swamis are examples of such a frame of mind.

We mustn't forget that the original meaning of swami is 'master' or 'prince'. It referred to becoming a master of oneself. Unfortunately, as always, those who will have accepted this premise, as in the then distant past, will be just the few, even as their needs will forever remain few. Physical needs. Some will call it mind over matter; others will just smile as though they held a common secret yet were unable to share it. While, as mentioned, in relation to the total number of inhabitants of our world such people will comprise but a small segment of the population, in relation to the population explosion, they'll still count in millions. Recessive though they might appear to be, all of them will have something in common. It will seem that happiness has become their intrinsic state of mind.

Yet, in the foreseeable future, not all will be quite as bright. Masses, as always, will remain the masses.

The vast majority of people will regard the few mentioned above as eccentric, as people deprived of education necessary to instill in them obedience to the dictates of the Big Brother. In fact, the Big Brother will not be that big. There will be nothing maga about the computer, but its countless units will be linked in a unifying, irrepressible network that will span the globe like a web of synapses through which electronic neurons will act as a single, almost divine entity.

In spite of bionic parts replacing most of human body and nano-particles cruising in its veins, people will refuse to define themselves as mechanical robots. They will insist they are human, a species superior to any other, though the resemblance to the old-time Homo sapiens will be mostly symbolic.

Some of them, or us, however, will look upon the man of the future as though we were mobile biological robots, rather than as men who once claimed to have been created in the image of his/her divine, if imaginary, creator. Nevertheless, the future man's potential will remain the same. Life will use any instrument, constructed of whatever material, as long as such instrument will retain the potential of sustaining a non-physical image of itself.

Just the potential. Hence hope is a necessary ingredient of survival.

Finally, it needs repeating that even after so many centuries, only the select few will begin to understand the sentiments expressed by ancient mystics.

The one good thing that will emerge out of 'evolution' will be that the majority of people will no longer be guided by invisible rings attached to their noses by the sacerdotal classes. Life will have become too comfortable for anyone to believe in gods, or devils, or heaven, or hell. They will be the true atheists, who will believe in god neither within nor without their being. They will be participating in the last stages of human devolution, holding on to last vestiges of humanity, living lives purely reactive to their environment. They will retain the ability to press buttons to satisfy all their needs. That will be all.

But they will not suffer. They will be unable to comprehend, to recall, that they had all once been, long, long ago, different forms of life. That is the true meaning of limbo.

Today, during the first few decades of the 21st century, there are pragmatic examples of the process of devolution in all walks of life. Throughout the world, tens of thousands of people are being treated like insubordinate cattle; they are herded at will at the end of a policeman's baton, subdued by a spray-can of pepper-spray, or rendered helpless by energy-directing weapons known as phasers. Until recently, the USA was proudly synonymous with the concept of individual freedoms. Even as I am writing this, the accelerated devolutionary process initiated by the past-president George W. Bush, has reached a new low. The present administration of the US has been forced to apologize, after the former 80-year-old Indian President APJ Abdul Kalam was frisked at a

New York airport. BBC Internet News reports that, although the protocol exempts former presidents and other dignitaries from such searches, this was the *second* time that Mr. Kalam has been subjected to such treatment.

The Press Trust of India (PTI) further comments on the dismal mental level of the security staff:

Mr. Kalam had already taken his seat on board the Air India aircraft. The security staff forced the crew to open the plane door, and then took away Mr. Kalam's jacket and boots because they had not done the necessary checks before boarding.

To be quite honest, I am against anyone being treated the way the USA treat their visitors. Or, for that matter, citizens of their own country. Their fear for their life has reached epidemic proportions. Since the reign of George W. Bush the concept of freedom, let alone respect, or even a smidgen of politeness, has taken a giant step backwards. I'd suggest that the nation as a whole is being punished not for electing the past-president, but for *re*-electing him.

This is but one example of devolution. There are countless others. There is also complete distortion of the concept of democracy.

Some years ago it has been said, that 1% of the populations, in the USA, owned 42% of the national wealth. Even more surprising is the fact that the bottom 80% of the populations held just 7%, leaving a whooping 93% to the remaining 20%.

Democracy?

Paradoxically, none of this appears to be accurate. It seems that China owns a good chunk of the US. They are said to hold reserves of some $3.5 trillion, of what used to be American money, on their side of the Pacific. China is, quite simply, the largest US bank. And they are not even asking to be bailed out!

Until recently Canada and Europe appeared to have

escaped this folly, although while writing this book, Europe fell under its own sword of Damocles. One is reminded of the biblical story of the seven fat cows. No one in today's western world seemed able to understand it.

As for the previous paragraph, it may or may not have been completely true. I'm not that good at math. But, as of today, and/or some years into the future, one thing is certain. Much, *much* less then 1% of the population will continue to evolve, spiritually, mentally, emotionally or even physically. We, North Americans, probably Europeans as well, continue to grow fatter, then obese, (excessive morbidity has been controlled by pills) more stupid, more selfish, more greedy, more lazy, more complacent, more... you fill in the rest, leaving yourself out, of course.

Doesn't it remind you of devolution?

Today, the remaining 99%+ of the population bear little resemblance to their distant forefathers, the Homo sapiens. They look and act more like *Homo Posterus*: a new species, slowly coming into its own, which appears to have absolutely no idea of where they are going. Not just in behaviour, but in appearance. Whatever the latest *mode du jour,* it is instantly swallowed, like yesterday's soup, and just as instantly becomes surgically transplanted to assure conformity. Such behaviour appears to give the masses a sense of belonging—to feel like a member of the new species.

A few years from now, wealthy plastic surgeons will make one look like anyone at all; most will choose the looks of the latest idol gallivanting across the large, 3D TV screens, adorning every room, every hall, every street-corner, and often every public restroom for those who dare to leave their secure castles in automated self-propelled, self-guided, self-steered conveyances. I am told that the surgical practice already flourishes in some areas of the Far East. People, mostly youngish women, seem to derive their pleasure and satisfaction from having been mistakenly recognized as the latest celebrity.

To each his, or on this case, her own? Such appears to be our future.

Then, in one of our tomorrows, as always, there will be the few who will carry on the heritage of the original species, once said to have been created with infinite potential. They will continue to look human. Not that others no longer will, but those few who will continue to exhibit rational behaviour, will remain immune to the dictates of the mass style.

Not many will be left, although even in North America 1% of, say, 320,000,000 people, (population projected for the USA by the time this book goes to print) is still 3,200,000 people. All we need do is make sure that we are among those few.

Yet, when all will have been said and done, when speculation will die down and the dust settles, and hoards of scientists will provide us with countless, often contradictory answers for just about any question under the sun, we, the remnants of the Homo sapiens, those few who have not devolved, shall never stop asking this question: Who am I?

There will be no rush. After all, we, in our consciousness, shall remain immortal, and time is but a figment of a scientist's imagination. We shall continue to evolve in an infinite succession of *nows*.

According to Socrates, the attempt to discover our real identity, our essence, should be of our first concern. It might also be the last. Although there is no beginning, and thus there can be no end. Everything else ensues from the answer we espouse. Not in the ultimate future, such also doesn't exist, but in the vital present. Basically, we are whatever we think we are. Individuals? Or will be—sooner or later.

Perhaps, it might be easier to attempt to define what we are not. Let us try.

As already established in Chapter 9, there are more bacteria than cells in a human body. Are the bacteria the real us? The real you and me? *Science Daily*, on the Internet, reports ten times as many bacteria in a human body as we have cells. If we ignore this fact, then we might care to count the atoms, although there's little point in this exercise as it has been proven and confirmed—yes, by scientists—that atoms are essentially empty space. Is this what we really are? Empty space? Or would we rather be bacteria. Is that what we really are? Hosts upon hosts of bacteria?

On the other hand, since the building components of our physical bodies are essentially empty space, perhaps we might be better off thinking of ourselves as bundles of energy. At least we could pretend that we generate some of the forces that seem to hold our universe together. But, if so, than what is it in us that controls those forces?

Compare us to our Milky Way. It contains 200-400 billion stars, perhaps upwards of 50 billion planets. A mere pittance in relation to the number of cells we hold in our private universes... in our bodies—not to mention the number of bacteria we support in our private... well you know, in our private world. Of course, it could just be that the bacteria are supporting us, that we are farms, which the bacteria cultivate to feed themselves. Not a very flattering proposition, but they are in the majority, so to speak.

Somehow I do not find either alternative particularly inspiring. Perhaps we are beginning to discover, slowly, what we are not? On the other hand, as we learned above, it's all—just about all—empty space.

So, once again, who are we?

***

Chapter 18
The God Diffusion

There is nothing more difficult to take in hand, more perilous to conduct, or more uncertain in its success, than to take the lead in the introduction of a new order of things.

Niccolo Machiavelli
Florentine political philosopher, historian, musician, and poet.
(1469—15270)

Perhaps is it time to change the word Diffusion to Confusion. While in the past the concept of God has been placed squarely in the realm of supernatural, high up in the sky, most certainly outside the reach of human beings, or even the bionically and nano-technologically enhanced humans of the future, we come daily face to face with divinity. Face to face with the powers that, the scientists say, created the world. Soon we shall come very close to God—to the instant of the Big Bang. That, to the scientists, will be as divine as one can get. Of course, the understanding what the word 'God' stands for has changed diametrically.

This might be the right place to review, once and for all, what the Bible has to say about God. There are many references, but four of them stand out above all others.

1. *I am that I am*
2. *Ye are gods.*
3. *Unto us a child is born...*
4. *I and my father are one.*

The first statement is attributed to Moses. When returning from Mount Sinai bringing with him the tablets with the Ten Commandments (please remember, most of this is shrouded in symbolism).

"*And Moses said to God, Behold, when I come to the children of Israel, and shall say to them, The God of your fathers has sent me to you; and they shall say to me, What is his name? What shall I say to them?*" (Exodus 3:13)

The answer is (in basic translation) loud and clear. "*I am that I am.*"

This statement may be dissected by theologians till kingdom come—unnecessarily. Seldom the Bible foregoes idiomatic language, and this is a glaring example of it. You may note that the deep symbolism is always omitted in places of extreme importance.

"I am not this I am, only that I am."

The vital point is that there is NO mention of god, or any other divinity. There is no Yahweh, no Jehova, no Elohim or Elah, or Eloah, or even just Jah. None of the above. Note the very conspicuous absence of any word that could be confused, even by the most ardent scientific atheists, with 'God'. "The name of your god is I am."

"I am has sent you. Not the I am you see with your physical eyes, but that other I am. That other I am that resides within you."

The second example: "*Ye are gods,*" is taken from Psalm 82:6 and is repeated in John 10:34. The meaning is self-evident, and to make sure no one can twist it in order to bamboozle the 'masses', there in an explanation: "…and all of you are children of the most High." Who is most High has been established by Moses. Now we must work to discover this state of consciousness within " I am".

The third example is given in Isaiah 9:6,
For unto us a child is born, unto us a son is given: and

the government shall be upon his shoulder: and his name shall be called Wonderful, Counsellor, The mighty God, The everlasting Father, The Prince of Peace.

The 'child' represents the onset of new consciousness, or new awareness. It is literally the new birth, but it refers to consciousness, not physical body, which the Bible never recognizes as the 'real' you. Progressive recognition of the power welling within us is expressed in beautiful, poetic language. For those interested, I recommend my *Dictionary of Biblical Symbolism*, where this particular and the following passages are translated into present-day language.

Finally, nothing can be clearer than the fourth example, "*I and my father are one.*" In this statement Yeshûa refuses to recognize any power outside his own being, or, more precisely, outside his own consciousness. Since he previously stated that we are all gods, one cannot but assume that we should all follow in his footsteps. This statement reminds me, once again of Jung's words, that individual is the only reality.

By Richard Dawkins's standards, Yeshûa defines himself as a committed atheist.

So much for atheists' gods of the Bible.

Now we can return to 'physical reality' knowing that we are in no danger of confusing it with the fundamentalists' misinterpretation of the Bible.

As mentioned in Chapter 15, computers will have passed the Turing Test in the near future.

In spite of that, Big Brother will never lay claims to divinity, which cannot be said of some people who will follow its dictates. They, the Big Brother's loyal subjects, will prefer to obey a 'higher' entity than one equal to them. The need of idols will remain in human psyche. Particularly in regressive or devolving psyche. It is much easier to take instructions from an infallible and thus 'divine' source than some sort of machine. Figure it out yourself.

With all their needs taken care of by Big Brother, the vast majority of people will have an awful lot of free time to fill with free thought. Many will have forgotten how to think altogether, but some, even the 'enhanced ones', will experience moments of clarity, in which they will be vaguely aware of missing something that seems very close, yet outside their grasp. For those few, there still will be a chance. A chance to evolve.

There is an old saying, still raising smiles from people with long memories, that magic is the science of the future. Well, exactly the same thing will happen to the word supernatural. What was once considered 'super' will be, in the future, accepted as ordinary. Thought-waves will become a measurable energy, more so than they already are today. Even computers, coordinated by Big Brother, will be proficient at various aspects of PK and ESP (psychokinesis and extrasensory perception), not to mention tunneling. (Quantum tunneling refers to the quantum mechanical phenomenon wherein subatomic particles tunnel through solid barriers, e.g. through a wall).

Regarding magic, I picked up an interesting tidbit on the BBC Internet news:

> Harry Potter's invisibility cloak may still be fantasy, but researchers are moving closer to making things disappear.
>
> At the Royal Society's Summer Science Exhibition in London, scientists make visitors gaze in amazement as small balls vanish before their eyes.
> This "invisibility stand" is one of the 22 projects being presented to the public this year.
> Among them are special glasses that help blind people 'see', tanks to capture sunlight and the so-called "smart traffic

control". The news report continued:

> Royal Society president Sir Paul Nurse told BBC News that the exhibition was a showcase not only for British science, but for the society in general.
> ...The project involving 'invisible' materials—called metamaterials—has attracted a lot of attention, with school children taking turns to hear the scientists explain the nature of the research.
> Metamaterials are materials unavailable in nature, in which the microstructure is changed to create unusual properties such as bending of electromagnetic waves.
> ...Professor Ulf Leonhardt of the University of St Andrews, one of the project leaders, told BBC News that in future, this technology could be applied in the areas of communications, wireless energy transfer, sensors and security.
> He said that the 'magic' illusion of disappearance stems from bending light in an unnatural way.
> "In the 'cloaking' device, you bend light around something so that you don't see the object, but you also don't see that the light has been bent—it enters the device in a straight lines and it also leaves the device in the same direction it came from, as if nothing had happened to it," he said.

The non-scientists can read more of the story at:
http://www.bbc.co.uk/news/technology 14084051 - story_continues_2
[Note: For human eyes, visible light falls between 380 to 750 nanometers. Most people are around this range; some may be able to see colours slightly above or below this range. The color of visible light waves depends on their wavelengths.]

And now, back to the **FUTURE**.

The concept that that which may have advanced beyond what had once been considered natural had to go through the process referred to as evolution will be long gone. Knowledge will be accepted to be omnipresent, rather like light in its infinite diversity of wavelengths. All we shall need to do to obtain it will be to enter our unconscious for the new, or subconscious for the past, and extract new wisdom or knowledge from within our psyche. And psyche, let us not forget, has long been recognized as the goddess of soul, as well to being synonymous with soul or spirit. It is not to be confused with the subconscious (*nephesh*), which in the Bible is often, erroneously, translated as soul.

Please note that I am describing ideas that will be explored by the few; not by the masses, which within a few decades will have regressed to quite primitive mental level.

After various religions will have shrunk to tiny conclaves holding on to past superstitions, some people, though childlike, will be learning, again, to stand on their own feet. They might takes as long as a few centuries for them to gain psychic freedom, which can be regarded as a period of apostasies.

"You cannot pour new wine into old skins..." people will remember, vaguely, as though through a fog of yesteryear. Yet the real teachings of the past will remain imbedded deeply in their psyche. Real teaching—time discarded as false by the misinterpretation of natural selection. Perhaps Darwin was right, after all, only his followers didn't understand him. Perhaps natural selection was intended to refer to human mind, not his or her body. Actually, Darwin didn't make it clear enough.

I wish I could believe it...

But Darwin's theory of natural selection may not be the only theory that may have been misinterpreted.

While, as I have already pointed out, the Bible has been

written in a highly symbolic idiom, making it virtually incomprehensible to fundamentalists—scientific and religious alike. Even when deciphered, though it then reads like guidelines for the living, the reader was not intended to regard himself as a product of biological evolution but as a spiritual being using the biological construct as a means to experience the process of becoming.

The biologists and their scientifically minded confreres who did not study symbolism, nor did they venture into the mystical nature of man, will, as far as the Bible is concerned, remain in the dark.

To cheer up the late developers who say that since the vast majority of people take the Bible literally, they cannot all be wrong, let me suggest an equal number does not understand quantum mechanics, yet not one of the stubborn scientific fundamentalists claims that therefore the quantum theory must be wrong. Furthermore, a number of biblical stories have been known long before biblical times, yet, in spite of the extended Kindergarten, they continue to be taken literally. It seems that indeed, many are called but few are chosen. The vast majority of people chose the easy way out, a way not requiring any effort or study, or hours of contemplation; they *choose* to remain ignorant.

Such people should not be that surprised when we consider that among the countless millions, now billions, of people, there are indeed very few to match Mozart, or Beethoven, or Verdi, or Shakespeare, or Yeshûa, or Buddha, or any of the giants of human species, exceptional or chosen people, who left those millions and billions behind. The ultimate consolation is that our true self is immortal, time a figment of our imagination, and ultimately we are all latent, dormant, if slightly retarded Buddhas.

Our time will come.

It seems that truth lies within us.
This inherent ability of the human species to access

virtually infinite knowledge that remains dormant in each one of us comes as a surprise to all, particularly to the scientists. They could never accept anything they couldn't measure. In most cases this ability still enjoys deep slumber—mostly in the minds of the recalcitrant fundamentalists.

I suspect that by the middle of the 3rd or 4th decade of the present century, most priests will be out of a job. With the incredible rise in the powers of computers, so will be most scientists. The tiny minority that will have resisted devolution will continue to recognize the infinite potential that lies within them. Those few will adopt 'stopping' as a daily mode of behaviour. This will become a catchphrase for meditation, contemplation, relaxation, but most of all for recharging one's inner batteries to increase the functionality of their brains. The select few will do so without the need of noisy loudspeakers, which in the past disturbed the peace from the tops of minarets, or church towers with their resonant bells, competing for the attention of the faithful. In the future, the reverse will be true. People will seek fulfillment within. Mostly, self-imposed silence.

For all who will practice moments of 'stopping', such moments will bring fruit beyond their wildest expectations.

That will be their secret. Silence. Total silence.

Not talking but listening. Stopping will mean more than just keeping quiet. One will have to still one's mind, one's thoughts, not just one's body. Silence will become a euphemism for worship, which word, for those people, will carry unpleasant connotation. Man will no longer bend his knee to anyone, to any image, any icon or idol. The chosen few will discover the power within. The rejuvenating and restoring as well as inspiring value of alpha waves, even for a short while, has been known for years.

On emerging from 'stopping', a new participator in the daily ritual will stand silent, surreptitious smile playing about his or her lips; they will seem surprised, unbelieving, yet accepting the evidence of their own inner senses. They will stand transfixed, open mouthed, galactic splendor still whirling in their eyes.

"Just then," they will say, "the universe and I became one. Can you believe it?"

They will.

***

Chapter 19
The Beginning of the End?

A democracy which makes or even effectively prepares for modern, scientific war must necessarily cease to be democratic. No country can be really well prepared for modern war unless it is governed by a tyrant, at the head of a highly trained and perfectly obedient bureaucracy.

Aldous Leonard Huxley, British author (1894—1963)

Many, many years into the future, after the best computers will prove unable to define infinity, some people will decide that while past and future are amusing subjects or hypotheses for entertainment, they will, henceforth, conduct their becoming in the Now. While they'll still use the concept of time in order not to allow all things happening at once, they'll also find that only *now* is what matters, and a succession of *nows* is as good a definition for infinity as anything they, or their computers, could think of. The succession of *nows* also took care of their need for becoming.

This, of course, will also take care of the Beginning *and* the End.

Not all agreed. The scientists (yes, they still fulfilled a function of categorizing discoveries made by people at large), and some (very few) priests, who will still desperately try to place the infinite outside the psyche of man, will remain on guard on the ramparts of fundamentalism. They will be treated with compassion, as one would children who, although showing promise, have not yet reached their maturity.

Yet, as always, the discovery of the 'now' will pertain only to individuals. To those few, who will consider themselves to be indivisible part of the Whole; of the omnipresent consciousness. The masses will continue to search for infinity outside their own being. On the fringes of the universe? Perhaps. I suspect they'd still call it god.

Just one problem will remain. If we were immortal, than how could we assure our means of fairly continuous becoming? Of the continuum of now?

In a purely physical sense, we hover on the thin line between living and dying all the time. Our bodies are continuously reconstructed, continuously rebuilt from elements that somehow become available for that purpose. We have biological evolution to thank for that. It seems that our physical renewal takes place partially from old cells breaking down, partly, possibly, from the food we eat. In the biological sense, this ongoing process we refer to as 'life'. What remains in question is our individuality. As we withdraw our consciousness from our physical bodies our consciousness appears to retain its characteristics, which define its uniqueness. Of one thing we can be sure. At any particular moment in our becoming, in any instant of now, we are the sum-total of everything we ever were; everything we had ever been. Physically, mentally and emotionally we carry our whole baggage in our genes. At mental level, it is all stored in our subconscious.

This may or may not be good news—depending on the baggage we carry. This concept, however, leads us to the unavoidable conclusion of recurrent reincarnation. Otherwise Wolfgang Amadeus Mozart couldn't possibly compose anything at the age of five. There are ample other examples which defy genetic explanation.

Paul Charles Morphy (1837—1884) who at just twelve years of age, defeated visiting Hungarian chess master Johann Löwenthal in a match of three games. Johann Carl Friedrich Gauss, was the son of poor working-class parents. Indeed, his mother was illiterate and never recorded the date of his birth. Nevertheless, Gauss was a child prodigy. There are many anecdotes pertaining to his precocity while a toddler, and he made his first groundbreaking mathematical discoveries while still a teenager.

Srīnivāsa Aiyangār Rāmānujan, (better known as Srinivasa Iyengar Ramanujan), was an autodidact (self-taught) Indian mathematician who, with almost no formal training in pure mathematics, made extraordinary contributions to mathematical analysis, number theory, infinite series and continued fractions. During his short life, Ramanujan independently compiled nearly 3900 results. The natural selection managed to kill him by the time he reached 32.

John von Neumann (1903—1957) was a Hungarian-American mathematician and polymath, who made major contribution in many fields. Hans Bethe, the Nobel laureate in physics once said, "I have sometimes wondered whether a brain like von Neumann's does not indicate a species superior to that of man". By the age of six, young John could exchange jokes in Classical Greek, memorize telephone directories on sight, and display prodigious abilities in mental calculations. As a 6-year-old, he astonished onlookers by dividing two 8-digit numbers in his head, and producing answers to a decimal point. By the time he was 8, he had attained mastery in calculus. The list goes on. Can natural selection explain that?

Baptized Pablo Diego José Francisco de Paula Juan Nepomuceno María de los Remedios Cipriano de la Santísima Trinidad Ruiz y Picasso, became known to us as Pablo Picasso. We also know him as Spanish expatriate, painter, sculptor, print-maker, ceramicist and stage designer.

Born in 25 October 1881, by 1893 the juvenile quality of his earliest work falls away, and at the age of 14, he painted *Portrait of Aunt Pepa*, a vigorous and dramatic portrait that Juan-Eduardo Cirlot has called "without a doubt one of the greatest in the whole history of Spanish painting." In spite of his dismally poor beginnings, neither environment nor natural selection had managed to kill him for 91 years. At the time of his death he owned some 50,000 works.

Saul Aaron Kripke, born on November 13, 1940, is an American philosopher and logician. He taught himself Ancient Hebrew by the age of six, read the complete works of Shakespeare by nine, and mastered the works of Descartes and complex mathematical problems before graduating elementary school. He wrote his first completeness theorem in modal logic at the age of 17, and had it published a year later.

The Internet adds to this list Ludwig van Beethoven, and a roster of more than 120 names of people who all reached maturity in their chosen fields before the age of 15, most a lot earlier. I am sure there are many more. It is amazing how many of them natural selection has mistaken for duds, and managed to kill off at a surprising early age.

Reincarnation, which would allow for knowledge to be passed on through other than just genetic means, seems like a very pragmatic explanation. By any scholastic standards known to man (or at least to me), none of the child prodigies listed above had sufficient time to acquire knowledge or expertise in their fields by the time they did. And this is not only a question of mental capacity; there is also the dexterity of Yehudi Menuhin's fingers who, at the age of 11, used them to perform the Beethoven's violin concerto. He previously played with the San Francisco Symphony orchestra at the age of 7. By the way, when Albert Einstein heard him a few years later, he is reported to have said, "Now I know there is a God!"

The reverse may be true, however. It may be that even the most talented child prodigies lose their uniqueness in later years. The natural selector or equalizer wins after all. Whatever the natural selection is capable of conveying, by whatever proxies or "phenotypic traits" they employ to "flesh out the anatomy, physiology, biochemistry or behaviour" (Dawkins's phrase), they obviously cannot pass on talent. Talent, let alone genius, seems in direct opposition to the natural selection powered by Darwinian replicators. Unless it happens by unwanted mutation, and if so, then it is quickly judged to be detrimental to the human species, and is quickly eradicated.

Surely, with such an abundance of inordinate talent, there would be at least some convincing evidence of genetic predisposition to quality on the side of parents or children of the wunderkind. Alas, there is none. Neither is there evidence that either the parents of the children exceeded the prodigy. It is becoming evident that natural selection concerns itself with physical survival only, even if it means reversal of progress ('devolution') to more primitive forms. Not a pleasant prospect, yet one that is becoming more and more visible in the behaviour pattern of the Homo sapiens.

There is an alternative.

The interesting aspect of the theory of reincarnation is that when we leave our physical bodies (people call this dying), our individualized consciousness retains all the characteristics it developed in its sojourn on earth (perhaps longer). A fringe benefit, and this is the nice part, that, providing our loved-ones, the so called dearly-departed, have not as yet constructed and entered another physical sheath (have not yet reincarnated), we have a good chance of not only meeting them, but actually recognizing them on the "other side" (in their disembodied condition). The wives can meet their husbands, the children their parents, and, of course, vice versa.

This could, on occasion, prove a very embarrassing

situation. But… Karma, it seems, does not stop here.

Of course, we need our physical bodies to be able to experience becoming. They provide us with the ability to experience contrasting emotions, consequences of positive and/or errant imagination, intellectual appreciation, as well as equip us with the five senses that we all take for granted. We tend to forget that it took us millions of years to evolve these attributes. Until we learn the architecture of our nature, we shall remain in the reactive stage of evolution, as are all animals, plants and even lower forms of 'life'.

What we do in the fragment of eternity between our reincarnations I leave to the mystics. The Buddhists seem to retire to Bardo. Perhaps they allow others there, too.

Unfortunately, once we return for another stint on earth, (or, perhaps, in anaerobic forms on other planets), the problem of recognition becomes very acute. To stop ourselves from going mad, we *temporarily* erase from memory our previous embodiments.

If any atheist can find a more pragmatic reality than that proposed above, then please, keep it to yourself. You probably deserve it. Anyone interested in pursuing this subject further can find my essay entitled *Immortality* in my *Beyond Religion* collections. I hope they'll enjoy it.

Galaxies apart, drifting, ever moving, billions, trillions of stars, clouds of stars still hesitant—in the process of formation, light, light pervading all, caressing, commanding, prodding, arranging, consciousness searching…

A universe of atoms, countless zillions of atoms, each atom a star, electrons whirling around them, ever new ones in a state of formation, constant formation, spinning, finding new relationships, new ways to serve, each on its prescribed journey, in its position in the universal order…

Clouds, countless clouds as yet invisible, but felt, timorous fragments of primeval energy, drifting, ever ready to take up their function, to take their righteous place in the universe, constantly in the state of formation, growing, expanding, renewing, ever alive...

Yes, the universes in a state of flux, drifting towards each other, then setting themselves apart, in constant communion, in a dance of joy, ever changing...

I am the consciousness of the universe.

World without beginning, without end...

I am a living god.

I AM THAT I AM.

Neither beginning nor end. Being and Becoming are one. Eternal.

I AM.

***

Chapter 20
Why We Shall Be: Phase Three

I'd rather entrust the government of the United States to the first 400 people listed in the Boston telephone directory than to the faculty of Harvard University.

William Frank Buckley, Jr.
American author and commentator, (1925—2008)

THE UNIVERSITY
(Incl. excerpts from Beyond Religion 1, Essay #52)

The biological answer is simple: we shall continue to be because our genes are immortal. As my friend said the other day, morons marry morons and produce more morons. But that is not really what I want to talk about. I wish to discuss reasons why we shall be what we shall be due to the evolution of our consciousness.

It may have escaped notice of some of my readers that the word university comes from Latin *universitas*, meaning the whole (world), or the universe. Hence, part three of our evolution, at least the evolution of some of us, and hopefully, ultimately, all of us. Let us never forget that we alone decide if we wish to be the chosen ones. Natural selection is concerned with physical survival and thus with quantity. The rest is up to us. Those of us who do decide to continue will have an effect on, and be affected by, the whole universe.

This may include any number of universes the scientists discover, as they go along. Perhaps as many universes as there are individualized states of consciousness.

I suggest that it should be made clear, that while in School the teacher has been, if often unsuccessfully, responsible for our learning process, in the University the onus lies squarely on our shoulders. We alone can decide if we wish to evolve, to continue evolving, and Darwin has very little to do with our progress. We are no longer relying on nature equipping us with the necessary appurtenances to get down from trees, to hunt for our prey (dinner), or even to combat the bacteria, viruses and a host of other bugs, which might threaten or enhance our wellbeing. To give credit where credit is due, most of us arrive at the university with a superb immune system. Nevertheless, by now we are intended to rely on our brain, mind if you prefer, to take care of our needs.

Regrettably, not every member of our species appears to know that, and they will pay the price for their ignorance. There is an old adage stating: "Ignorance of the law is no excuse for breaking it." This law applied throughout our evolution, voluntarily or imposed on us by nature, and/or by the universal laws. Regretfully, also by those who take it upon themselves to subjugate those they think weaker than they are. Let us never forget that, more often then not, bad governments are elected by good people who don't vote. Thus, responsibility reverts to us.

We must also never forget the biblical statement that many are called but few are chosen. Mother nature is cruel. Not every acorn will grow into an oak tree. Not every seed will bear fruit. Not every member of the Homo sapient species will reach his or her intended potential. That's how nature works: in incredible abundance, in the hope that at least some of her plans will be fulfilled. We know that our bodies are recycled. Who knows what happens to our individualized states of consciousness? We know that they are immortal, but can they return to their Source, even as every drop of rain will, ultimately, return to the Ocean? Furthermore nature is most absurdly wasteful, or generous, if you hold God or Darwin responsible for creation. Sometime ago, an article from the *Washington Post* has been reprinted in my local newspaper. It has announced the results of an extensive scientific research, which stated that: *"Most newly conceived human embryos harbor colossal genetic defects that are incompatible with life."* Furthermore, *"...most pregnancies—whether naturally occurring or the result of test-tube fertilization—quietly fail within days or a few weeks after conception."*

That's only a small part of it. Yet in *God Delusion* Dawkins writes:

"Religion is so wasteful, so extravagant; and Darwinian selection habitually targets and eliminates waste. Nature is a miserly accountant, grudging the pennies, watching the clock, punishing the smallest extravagance."

Please read on. It seems that Messrs. Darwin and Dawkins live on a different planet.

An average (human) male produces between two and six milliliters of semen in each ejaculation. This adds up to between 200 and 500 million sperm cells. Let us accept a conservative average of 300 million cells. Multiply that by say, 2 billion males, then by, say, 52 ejaculations per year. Do your own math.

300,000,000 x 2,000,000,000 x 52 = the number of sperm cells wasted by males of our species alone in a single year. Less the successful impregnations, of course—one per year per male, say. For a few years. Then? Zilch!

On the other hand we should add, perhaps, the same 2 billion men, boys really, going through their teen masturbatory years. That should add a good few trillion wasted sperm cells. After all, nature disposes teenagers by *very natural selection* to do so, right? Naturally, the boys might prefer to select girls, but usually they are not given a chance.

Surely, my figures are *very* conservative, yet wastage is staggering by any standard. By contrast, women produce but a few eggs at a time, but even then, most go by the wayside. They are also wasted. The profusion of nature's squander is flabbergasting. Perhaps in another few million years it will improve its batting average. At present, nature's idea of Pragmatic Realism is to produce everything in such abundance that at least some of them are going to work—the most primitive trial and error technique.

"...punishing the smallest extravagance???"

I presume—by habitually destroying it's own creation. Don't get me wrong. I do not disagree with natural selection. I do disagree with juxtaposing it to religion in any way whatsoever. Perhaps nature ought to listen to Mies van der Rohe who advocated the maxim that "less is more". He was also talking about creation; only he referred to buildings.

And then, Dawkins adds on the same page:

"Nature cannot afford frivolous *jeux d'esprit*."

My goodness! At the risk of being frivolous, I read somewhere that, with regards to masturbation, there are only two types of men in the world. Those who admit to doing so, and those who don't admit it. That leaves, say, 3 billion men who do (the rest of the population are women and children). Let us multiply this number by some 300 million sperm at each ejaculation, and then say, again, by (a minimum?) of 52 weeks per year, and we have an elegant image of nature's idea of *jeux d'esprit*.

This seems to fall somewhat short of the "traditional interpretations of Darwinism, in which 'benefit' is assumed to mean benefit for individual survival and reproduction".

Unless, of course, Darwin and Dawkins exclude the human species from the evolutionary equation. Wouldn't that be interesting?

Just to recap. To make Pragmatic Realism work in the evolutionary sense, nature has devised a system referred to by Charles Darwin and his followers as natural selection. The system relies on its self-perpetuation, on the production of sperm/seed/acorn in such a profusion, with such abandon, that at least one sperm/seed/acorn might be malformed, which in turn might result in a mutation, which, if it survives, which is doubtful, might result in... an evolutionary advancement.

Or not. Or it might prove inferior to *status quo*.

Of course, some seed/acorns might be eaten by other wasteful organisms. As for human sperm, no one in their wildest dreams could accuse nature of exhibiting even a smidgen of intelligence in its method. Unless... ...unless, regardless of what nature does with the rest of her creative profusion, from the evolutionary point of view, our, human, sole purpose, is to serve as milking cows for the bacteria, who, or which, indulge their gustatory tastes in the epicurean delight of our sperm.

The rest of the time, we can walk about picking up poop after our dogs. (If you want to find our true purpose in the canine reality, I refer you to *"Broohos"* in my *Cats and Dogs* stories.)

We, you and I, are part of nature. At least physically. For some of us, that's all we are. Wasters? Or are we, some of us, more than that?

At the University stage, we become students. We discover that our newly found freedom is commensurate with our acceptance of responsibility. We no longer hold teachers, preachers, priests, confessors, psychologists, politicians, our parents, or even circumstances, responsible for our survival. In fact, our definition of survival is undergoing a fundamental change. The extension of our physical life is no longer our priority. Quality takes preference over quantity. We begin to suspect, then know, that we are entities with an unimaginable potential. We learn from every quarter, from the past and the present, from nature, from the positive and negative traits still integral to our mental, emotional and physical embodiments. We learn the difference between reactive and causative action. We refuse to conform for the sake of the illusion of security we used to derive from the concept of belonging. We become individuals.

Even as the preceding phases of our evolution dealt with survival within constraints of time and space, they were also confined to specific duration. Our university, however, deals with that which has neither beginning nor end. It finds its reality outside constraints of the space/time continuum. This realization empowers us to step outside our material constrains. Outside our physical bodies. From this new vantage point we observe the forces controlling our environment. We observe the rich becoming richer, the poor––poorer. Only we no longer measure wealth by the old yardstick of money or fame or power. Those who are happy––increase in their joy, the miserable—tend to sink into depression. *Regardless of circumstances.* We became aware of the universal rule that, unwittingly, controlled us from the moment we became enwrapped in material reality:

**WE ARE THE PRODUCT
OF OUR CONTEMPLATION.**

We note that every thought we entertain influences our environment. Every thought we energize with emotion, defines our future. We learn to control our thoughts. We become selective in the use of, and learn to control, our emotions. We learn that to realize a dream, we must have a dream. To reach a goal, we must have a goal. To realize the impossible, we must believe that *everything* is possible. We become the conscious effect of the creative power of our beliefs. We perceive that at every instant of existence, we are the consequence of our past, the forerunners of our futures.

DELUSIONS 187

We take control. Growing we grow, maturing we mature, ever reaching for the eternally receding horizon. Slowly, so very slowly, it dawns on us that there are no horizons. We realize that we, ourselves, define the characteristics and the scope of our reality. We realize that we create the universe in which we find our being. The lightening strikes. Time stops. We begin living in the present.

There may be another mode to our existence. As the universe seems to be almost empty of matter, we may find, in time, the secret of the great mystics of the past.

(see POSTCRIPTUM)

What if the whole universe, including our human bodies, were to be the result of the creative energy (spirit, if you like) unfolding itself in a pragmatic way? What if it were an ongoing process that seems to have had neither a beginning, nor a predictable end? All manner of creation is endowed with the ability to act in accordance with the universal laws, inherent in the creative energy itself. It is discernible in all, including human animals. We begin in a reactive mode of becoming. And then "unto us a child is born." This is a wondrous phrase, already discussed above (Chapter 18), in which the prophet Isaiah describes his own experience. I beg your indulgence to look at it once more:

> "For unto us a child is born, unto us a son is given: and the government shall be upon his shoulder: and his name shall be called Wonderful, Counsellor, The mighty God, The everlasting Father, The Prince of Peace."

Let us examine this phrase in detail. The 'child' symbolizes the first awareness that we may, just may, be more than just flesh and bones. This thought alone grows into such confidence that, instead of listening to priests and other men of authority, we begin to trust our own self. We no longer defer to outside sources to know how to act. As our confidence rises still further, we begin to realize that this power that has awakened within us is quite inexplicably wonderful. We began to trust in our judgment not just in decision concerning our everyday affairs, but also in matters of greater and greater importance; in matters affecting the welfare of others; of our whole environment. Even as we learn to do so, even as our confidence grows, we feel the stirring of unlimited power welling within us. We feel that nothing is impossible for us. And then, surprisingly, we realize that this power was always dormant within us, and that it is that power and not what we thought we were, that brought about this change within us. We begin to suspect that this authority, this ability, was always there, only it took us a long time to realize it, and then accept it. It and we became inseparable, indistinguishable. We became one. In the next phase, we realized that, in fact, we always were one. And this immutable knowledge gives us a most extraordinary, unearthly feeling of peace. Peace beyond human understanding.

The perceiver and the perceived became one.

Actually, they always were. Whether one reaches this realization in ones present life, or a million years from now, it matters little. That which waits dormant within us is immortal. It has its being outside the confines of time and space. It changes its external sheath until a suitable one is ready. Then, and only then this euphoric union takes place.

So said Isaiah some 2700 years ago. One can but wonder how many people listened.

This process described so poetically by the Prophet Isaiah should never be confused with the condition described by the American psychologist, Julian Jaynes, which he also appears to associate with the growth of human consciousness. In his observations there are external voices that insinuate themselves into our heads and imbue us with a reality supported by such voices, sometimes accompanied by hallucinatory images. The condition he describes is reminiscent of schitsophrenia or some other deeply seated psychosis.

The above statement by the Prophet Isaiah has nothing to do with such images, sounds, or explanations. Any externalization, or dichotomy, taking place at any stage of the growing realization of our true nature would immediately throw us into the waiting arms of the religious proselytizers. We would immediately fall into the clutches of religion. The only method of reaching the state of consciousness offered by Isaiah is a lonely, lonesome, individual journey. No two people can reach the same level of realization of the infinite. That is why, perhaps, there are so many of us, scattered throughout the universes.

But we should have no delusions.

Those who are not even aware of the wondrous child, of the potential dormant within us—Yeshûa called dead. But there is hope. They are not already dead, but *still* dead. Not yet awakened. Like Buddhas in waiting.

Considering that the man who is describing his new awareness is said to have lived between 759 and 690 BC, his evolutionary level vastly exceeded most men I've met to this day. He obviously states that, with a little effort, we can reach out towards our infinite potential. The only god he recognized was within his consciousness. Yeshûa of course, reiterated the same sentiment later. People, religionists, churches and… scientists, continued to look for that infinite potential outside their own being. Hence, disappointment and abject deism or atheism—two sides of the same coin.

According to Isaiah, this new state of consciousness is making us aware that we are each, individually, one and inseparable from the total, universal, omnipresent consciousness, which brings about the transient state of eternal becoming. This new consciousness, this new awareness, this new 'child' is one and indivisible from the omnipresent consciousness.

Fraction of the infinite is still infinite. All the attributes are the same. They are indivisible.

All the knowledge is already within us. It is only a question of recall.

***

Chapter 21
Scientist's Delusion

*"Tell him to live by yes and no — yes to everything good,
no to everything bad."*
As quoted in *The Thought and Character of William James* by
Ralph Barton Perry

"Let your Yea *be* Yea; *and your* Nay, Nay.*"*
Matthew 5:33

For some reason my favourite writer on all matters pertaining to biology fails to realize that admitting to being an agnostic, though with profound leaning towards atheism (apparently his mental stance of choice), simply lays claim to being ignorant, at least in the realms of matters discussed. And ignorant Dr. Dawkins most emphatically is not, providing he sticks to the illustrious subject of his expertise. To biology. It is true that his erudition in literature is quite exemplary, and his knowledge of various scriptures, the Bible in particular, surpasses that of most 'believers', but his heart does not seem to lie in it. Perhaps he just cannot serve two masters. Essentially, though denying this fact, all the interpretations of scriptures I read in his book are *exclusively* fundamentalist. Pity. His wonderful acumen and extensive knowledge could contribute a great deal to the truth veiled in those documents.

Perhaps, taking into account that we, humans, are still extremely primitive units of awareness, agnosticism may be the most honest admission of ignorance. Although it may also, on occasion, act as a slight stimulus, it seldom advances the cause of learning. One doesn't hear people saying, "I'm agnostic about the intangible, because I know nothing about it". Nor, with the exception of speculative theoreticians, have I met many scientists who were willing to forsake their acquired knowledge, in order to cross new horizons. Even Einstein wasn't willing to accept quantum mechanics. Rather one hears, "I'm an agnostic and proud of it. It's the only honest thing to be." For them, apparently, ignorance is bliss.

Agnosticism is not an end in itself but, at best, a means to escape drawing conclusions. The usual admission sounds more like a coffin nail in ones brain than a stimulus to expand ones consciousness. And, when all is said and done, considering that life is the essence of change, and that our world is filled exclusively with at least possibilities, and for the daring among us with probabilities, the only thing that is worthwhile is the trip.

The journey itself.

Since Thomas Huxley, another English biologist, coined the term in 1869, the term agnostic has been used almost exclusively by scientists, who may have had reasons not to confess their atheism openly. What baffles me is that the essence of agnosticism has been used in, what can only be termed as religious writings, namely by Nasadiya Sukta in Rig Veda, the Sanskrit text written c.1700–1100 BC. Yet, more often then not, it is used against religious thought, rather than to support it. In the light of what the majority of churches have done with various myths, I can hardly blame those people, but it would be nice if a scientist, somewhere, had the courage to show the folly of 'modern' religion, rather than the folly of faith. I am fully aware of many evils that may have been fuelled by the power of faith. Yet faith, hope and charity are prerequisites to our survival. Physical and—if you think of yourself as more than 27^{30} near empty space atoms whirling in near emptiness—otherwise.

So, let us not delude ourselves. To repeat, we are stardust thinly diluted in bags of water, pretending to know something. We don't, but it's such fun pretending, isn't it? Some say that, unbeknownst to many, with the onset of the Industrial Revolution we, the human race, have entered the Age of Aquarius. Without venturing into the inner meaning of the Procession of the Zodiac, enough said (by the ancient Hindus) that the Age of Aquarius will last some 2150 years, during which time we are to become (more) self-reliant. That is not to say that we are to close our eyes to external sources of knowledge, but that we must learn discrimination in our judgment. We shall no longer be able to blame others for our misfortunes. Not even science or scientists.

In his book *The God Delusion*, Richard Dawkins discusses a "trickle down theory of creation." Then, scrupulously, honest that he is, he denies the authorship of the 'theory', and appears to give full credit for it, equally to Darwin and, apparently, to his late friend, philosopher Daniel Dennett.

"You'll never see a spear making a spear maker. You'll never see a horseshoe making a blacksmith. You'll never see a pot making a potter."
Then he adds:
"The concept of stunning simplicity that he (Dennett?) was talking about was, of course, nothing to do with me. It was Darwin's theory of evolution by natural selection—the ultimate scientific consciousness raiser."
Finally Dawkins adds one more tidbit:
"Darwin's discovery of a workable process that does that very counter-intuitive thing is what makes his contribution to human thought so revolutionary, and so loaded with the power to raise consciousness."

Does it mean that a pot *does* make a potter? A spear *is making* a spear maker? My consciousness is having problems following the logic. There is logic there, somewhere, isn't there? I suspect he merely means that small, simple things are capable of combining to make complex structures. Or at least, that's how I understand Darwin, without all the rigmarole.

Unfortunately the observations are not taken to a logical conclusion. Before I began writing, I spent many years practicing architecture. The reverse "trickle down theory" can, in a way, be applied to my old profession. I noticed, that I'd never seen a building before the architect produced the working drawings. The working drawings could not be produced until the design has been produced. And the design could not be presented to the client until the architect had an idea what to draw. Thus, the "trickle down (or up?) theory" proves that the *idea* precedes "anything physical" taking place.

The idea, that elusive, intangible, ethereal concept, must come first.

By simple logic we must conclude that the mind precedes the brain, which in turn we employ to translate an idea into an object, which we can share with others in the objective reality.

Pragmatic Reality demands it of us.

And talking of Pragmatic Realism, there is that gently nagging problem of evolution.

Frankly, from the Pragmatic Realism point of view, it is a matter of relative indifference to me whether the world, as we know it, began with the influence of "objects of worship", or in a primordial cesspool. What matters to me is which theory can make me a better man today. As you may have noticed, I am an advocate of living in the present.

Discounting extraterrestrial *accidental* bombardments, (grudgingly admitted as a possibility even by evolutionary biologists), there are two basic theories concerning the origins of life. (No, not the fundamental creationists' nonsense). The first proposes the theory that could be described as *many resulting in few*, and the second as *few evolving into many*. Also the first is concerned, principally, with quality—the second with quantity. The differences are mostly philosophical, and/or pragmatic, although the word evolution has a slightly different meaning.

The first is the biblical model, wherein 'objects or worship' (extraterrestrials, though not necessarily organic life-forms) originated evolution on Earth, which 'they' hoped would ultimately result in a few good evolutionary products. "Many are called, few are chosen" would fit in nicely into this theory. Please note, evolution remains unscathed—it is still evolution.

The second theory is the Darwinian model, wherein the few (proteinoids, or thermal proteins formed inorganically from amino acids, were the precursors of the first living cells) would, eventually, result in (great, great) many living organisms.

I don't think either theory will change my plans for dinner, tonight. Or what tie I'll wear tomorrow. Even my distant cousin, the biologist, will probably not change his thesis about what his parasites feeding on the excrement of bats had for dinner last night. There is, however, just one stimulus hidden in one of the theories: that nagging phrase that, "Many are called and few are chosen." I find it stimulating to try my best to make the right choices throughout my life, regardless of my origins. The Darwinian model offers me no such stimulus. And let us not forget, I'm talking only about the origins—the rest remains the same. The only theory that has any effect on me today is Pragmatic Realism. The rest is just, "Much ado about (almost) nothing".

At long last we come to the essence of the delusion propagated by science. Before we dismiss science, as many scientists dismiss religions, shouldn't we ask ourselves how many of the 7 billion people crowding our Earth have benefited from the knowledge that a proton consists of two up-quarks and one down-quark? On the other hand, such knowledge may have brought us closer to the invention and production of an atomic bomb. While religious misinterpretations of scriptural teaching are certainly responsible for many a wholesale slaughter, no religion or its misbegotten promulgators have ever threatened the existence of life on Earth. (At least, not yet). Science, specifically nuclear science, did. Actually, still does. As I am sure might a number of artificial bugs, which the biologists are on the verge of discovering.

And if you think that I am going too far, then think of the hydrogen bombs. They are much more destructive. Or, better still, think of the 30,000 bombs presently stored by various military regimes (including the USA), under strict supervision of... scientists, of course. The detonation of a few well placed such installations could easily put an end to humanity on Earth as we know it.

And if anyone were to survive a few well-placed mistakes, the evolutionary biologists would be rejoicing. The nuclear radiation would result in countless mutations. At last progress, the evolutionary biologists would cry! At long last nature would have a field day, or century, or millennium, to make her almost-natural selections.

No matter; perhaps the next holocaust will vindicate Roger Fouts and Stephen Tukel Mills, in their prophetic book: *Next of Kin: My conversations with Chimpanzees*, suggesting that we are not the pinnacle of evolution, but only a rather unsuccessful branch of the major stem of Chimpanzees. I don't really mind. I never met a Chimpanzee I didn't like, which I cannot say about their next of kin.

So much abortive evolution; so much waste...

At least religions convert, or used to convert, most of their money into art. The scientists... you decide? And talking of the money aspect.

Science Daily (Dec. 13, 2006) reports: — A group of 50 international physicists, led by UC Riverside's Ann Heinson, has detected for the first time a subatomic particle, the top quark, produced without the simultaneous production of its antimatter partner—an extremely rare event. The discovery of the single top quark could help scientists better explain how the universe works and how objects acquire their mass, thereby assisting human understanding of the fundamental nature of the universe.

Wouldn't it be nice if the scientists discovered a cure for the common cold? Now they are saying the same thing about the Higgs boson.

Just think—50 international physicists! And, having spent countless millions of dollars of public funds, (or pounds, or rubbles, or franks, or rupees, or yuans...) to find the top quark, after they discover its mass, they'll learn that that mass is surrounded by mostly empty space. And next time they might not be so lucky. They might stumble across a bunch of antimatter particles. Bingo, or perhaps Little Bang? Look, no scientists! Just more empty space.

It has been said that science is always better than ignorance. I put it to you that ignorant scientists are more dangerous than ignorant priests. Their toys are more dangerous. But to give priests their due, I should add the following to balance the odds.

Dawkins writes that:

"...a Gallup poll in the United States of America found the following. Three-quarters of Catholics and Protestants could not name a single Old Testament prophet. More than two-thirds didn't know who preached the Sermon on the Mount. A substantial number thought that Moses was one of Jesus' twelve apostles."

I am surprised they could count to twelve. But in their defense, I'd rather hear *what* it was that Yeshûa was preaching on the Mount. Not *who* was preaching. What really counts is the message, not the messenger.

All the same, is this the "American culture" they're so keen to export around the world? This and hamburgers, American Idols, and Hollywood miasma? Well, at least they have more atom bombs than anyone in the whole wide world.

I have a number of very, very good dear friends in America, and they are as embarrassed as I am.

I am also very close to giving up. If only the scientists would allow me to keep faith that this present (imaginary?) reality is only temporary. That one day we shall all wake up and find ourselves in another Golden Age.

At long last, a word about Pragmatic Reality.

To listen to biologists, one gets the impression that nature, in her wisdom, looks dispassionately at a vast array of choices and then makes a profound selection of the best traits necessary for a gene to survive. This is not how nature operates. From the "natural selection" point of view, the method is simple: *If it ain't broke, don't fix it.* In fact the greatest effort nature appears to make is in maintaining the *status quo*. Like all forces that wield power, the churches, the governments, the oligarchies and, the most powerful oligarchy of all: nature.

Cockroaches and sharks are two of the examples that come to mind. Fossils indicate that cockroaches have been around for at least 340 million years. They seem omnipresent, and survive in great many environmental conditions, including north and south poles, at 670 meters depth of coalmines, and will survive 2 weeks without food, while an A4 piece of paper will feed one for a week.

As for sharks, "fully 350,000,000 years ago, sharks had evolved a reproductive strategy which favors the production of a small number of offspring, retained, protected, and nourished within the body of the mother, and requiring a strong investment of the female's time and resources." (So says *Pacific Fisheries Coalition* on the Internet).

If, Darwin and Co. are concerned with evolutionary survival, then their selective process needs look no further. Humans have a lot to learn from both, cockroaches and sharks. Evolutionarily speaking, they are both more successful than we are. More advance that Homo sapiens.

What minute and extremely rare changes do occur in "natural selection" that might result in an evolutionary upward step are invariably the result of a 'mistake', which the evolutionary biologists call mutations. When something goes wrong with the self-perpetuating/replicating process of a gene, a tiny slip, *and* nature doesn't notice it until it's too late to be instantly destroyed, then a change might indeed take place, and a new, accidental gene might—again accidentally—prove to have greater survival value than its predecessor. Usually any deviation from the established norm is caught in time and eliminated, as in the human reproductive process—see Chapter 20, above.

And this, the evolutionary biologists call natural selection. Sorry, Charles, but it sounds more like wholesale murder.

Finally a word about raising of our consciousness.

There is a compendium of books called the Bible, whose sole purpose is to help us to raise our consciousness. Should anyone wish to forego the fundamentalist nonsense and attempt to decipher this document, this collection of documents, to discover their symbolic meaning, (which protects the wisdom from 'unholy eyes'), I offer, once again, my *Dictionary of Biblical Symbolism*. It is more than evident that the scientists are in dire need of it. They might, just might actually find that Yeshûa was the greatest atheist of them all. He certainly disliked the sacerdotal class of his day.

As for the symbolism employed in the Bible, the following warning is issued for obvious reasons.

"Give not that which is holy unto the dogs, neither cast ye your pearls before swine, lest they trample them under their feet, and turn again and rend you." (KJV, Matthew 7:6).

There is a reason for it. A consciousness raised above their fellow men wields enormous power. In the hands (heads, minds) of those who have not yet established high ethical standards could be disastrous for others. Remember, consciousness, like spirit or life, are *neutral*. It is us, you and I, who can use it or abuse it. "All power is given to the son."

There are examples of this.

Attempting to raise consciousness without defining what we mean by the term is, to say the least, abortive.

On the other hand, we need three known, accepted, proven qualities of man's psyche to examine the world we live in, in terms of Pragmatic Realism. The *Conscious*, the *Subconscious* and the *Unconscious*. In terms of these three states of consciousness we can define our reality.

In the New Testament, the *unconscious* corresponds to the 'biblical father', the omnipresent intelligence, the omnipresent creative force, often referred to as spirit, life force, and presumably referred to by Darwin as Universal Laws, though the latter sounds like a limiting definition. The *unconscious* is the source from which all that is unmanifested comes into manifestation. Intangible, even as the *unconscious*, is the *conscious*, referred to in the Bible as its 'son', and thus indivisible from the *unconscious*. The *conscious, as the* individualization of the *unconscious*, exemplifies life or, the condition of change and thus becoming, while the *unconscious* represents the (infinite) potential i.e. the static condition.

The *subconscious* is little more than memory storage of that which already took place. It does, however, maintain the *status quo*. It uses its acquired knowledge and records all new tidbits of information. That is why it tends to reproduce the malignant cells, which should be replaced *not* reproduced. To replace them, however, a creative (not reproductive) act must take place. The *conscious* must reprogram (contemplation, meditation or autohypnosis may be used), the reproductive program, so that the 'replacement cells' do not repeat the known knowledge, but the improved one. A sort of conscious natural selection.

The *conscious*, or the biblical I AM, is the boss. It makes all the judgments, decisions, definitions of what is required. On rare occasions it can reach out to the *unconscious* (e.g. during contemplation), in search of possibilities. Yeshûa describes the relationship (generically) between the *conscious* and the *unconscious* as that of son and father. Usually the *unconscious* is taken to be replete with a vast array of possibilities (the *unconscious* is non-judgmental), and the *conscious* must still decide what is best, but at least new fields or possibilities are opened. In this way, the *conscious* and the *unconscious* are inseparable. As mentioned above, the *conscious* is the individualization of the *unconscious*, with the added attribute of self-awareness.

Thus, to quote Jung once again, the "Individual is the only reality."

There is a great deal of confusion regarding various states of consciousness. So to sum up, there is *I AM*, as indicted above, which defines our state of being, and *I AM*, which describes our state of becoming. The two are inseparable hence virtually—one.

By the mere fact that the *unconscious* is endowed with the attribute of individualizing itself, does not make any part of it any less than Whole. It is rather like arguing how many souls there are. In the I AM sense, there is but one, spelled with a capital S. I AM is the attribute of the *unconscious* to individualize itself.

'I AM', (as in I AM that I AM) also describes our transient condition of becoming. I am happy, I am sad, I am an architect, writer, dancer, singer, physician, and so forth.

There seems to be also a great deal of confusion between the biblical concept of 'soul' and the subconscious that is the indispensable part of our psyche. Up to the first breath taken by the baby, human or otherwise, the gestation is dependant exclusively on the data stored in our genetic system, which corresponds to our subconscious. In fact, the Hebrew word for the *subconscious* is '*animal soul*', representing the passive side (the non-creative) of our psyche, and which is erroneously translated and confused with the Soul, which represents I AM. The fundamental difference is that soul, *nephesh*, or the 'animal soul', defines our differences. I AM, or the individualized Soul (note the capital letters), defines what makes us one.

Of course, the *unconscious* manifests only through its creation, the *conscious*, according to the capacity of the individualized creation to receive the influx from the *unconscious*. It was well expressed by Thomas Aquinas: *Whatever is received is received according to the nature of the recipient.*

This is certainly true not only of human nature, but of the rest of fauna and flora; however, it appears that only humans are capable of appreciating the indivisibility of their own consciousness from the unconscious—although very few humans, at that. Most have no idea who they are, and if they believe in a god, then it is usually a god with their own traits magnified and assigned to him or her. The Greeks illustrated this thesis extremely well in their Pantheon, the Romans copied it quite faithfully, and other religions compromised the system by pretending to create monotheism, and then dividing it into 3 or more parts. The scientists, often unbeknownst to them, often come up with new ideas first thing in the morning, most probably as a result of immersing themselves in the unconscious during their sleep. Whether they believe in it or not is of absolutely no consequence. To repeat the words of Yeshûa, "the father (the unconscious) judges no man, but has committed all judgment unto the son."

DELUSIONS 203

In you and me, that's our conscious awareness.

Now, a word about 'things' just as invisible as atoms, yet, to vast number of people, just as real. For many years, a number of institutions of higher learning have been busy researching PK and ESP. Those magic letters stand for Pure or Psychokinesis, sometimes referred to as telekinesis, and Extra Sensory Perception. There is nothing supernatural about any of these, and we all know that magic is the science of the future. No group of fundamentalists among the scientists will stop human progress. I am not talking about the devolving masses. I am talking about the select few. Do you remember? Many are called, but few are chosen. Once again the ominous words seem to apply to our present situation.

The research in matters reaching beyond our physical senses is carried out, among other places, in Princeton, Harvard and Duke Universities in the US; the University of Northampton and Cambridge, in the UK; in Moscow and Odessa State Universities; and *many* other, similar groups have been formed in such countries as Holland, Sweden, France, and Greece. I'm sure more research would yield even more results.

All this research is conducted by *scientists*, usually with Ph.D.s added to their names. Should 'other' scientists of both pure and applied sciences take them seriously? Or should the fundamentalists among them lump them together with theologians and dismiss them as... as what, superior beings, or inferior intellects?

Dogmatic fundamentalism is a terrible disease. Often it affects most excellent intellects.

Once again the phrase, "I make all things new", comes to mind, only now we must search much deeper. This is what Krishnamurti had to say about turning over a new page. "You can renounce a few cows, a house, but to renounce your heredity, your tradition, the burden of your conditioning, that demands an enormous inquiry".

That is what the future NOW is for. To make all things new. To find new means for crossing bridges that had not been built as yet. To dare to walk, where others do not dare. It means reaching out where others fear to tread. Like Captain James Tiberius Kirk, and his band of merry men—just like in the Sherwood Forrest. Or in a laboratory where people are not afraid for their ego.

Usually, inventions are the products and achievements of lazy people. Technology of the future will enable man to delegate 90% of his efforts to computerized machines. Man, *en masse*, swamped by excessive leisure time will grow progressively more lazy, stupid and useless.

So much for evolution as conceived by scientists. Perhaps what matters is the evolution of our mind, of spirit—the existence of which they often deny. Esoteric Buddhism foretold the future with uncompromising honesty. Perhaps, we should heed its admonitions.

Finally it is time to introduce a concept that seems strange to the world of science, although it is relatively simple. Let us pretend (or accept) that the world really is virtually empty space. Let us pretend, just this once, that the scientists are right. That Sir Arthur Eddington wasn't drunk when he declared that matter is essentially empty space.

Instead, let us fill this seemingly empty space with something.

With what, you might well ask?

The easy answer would be with intelligence, with imagination, with thoughts; let us flood the universe with love. Unfortunately the mystics will tell us that this has already been done, by *their* version of God. So how can we reconcile the divine with the material? There is only one grain of hope left.

How about with energy? What energy? With light. With photons.

With particles that having no mass they appear to us, to our scientists *and* most probably to people steeped in religion, as empty space. If you like the idea, read on.

***

POSTSCRIPTUM

Men are so simple and so much inclined to obey immediate needs that a deceiver will never lack victims for his deceptions.

Niccolo Machiavelli
Florentine political philosopher, historian, musician, and poet.
(1469—15270)

There is only one thing that separates us from all the other life forms, and that is our ability to choose. The rest of life forms are reactive. We, and we alone, can say no. We can, if we choose, be proactive. But this entails consequences. It was fun *Climbing Mount Improbable*, but the time may be coming to say goodbye to being biological robots designed to feed our DNA. The future sounds fascinating—an infinity of unknowns. And one of them, as I'm sure Kurzweil would agree, is that we might soon be replaced by thinking, mobile computers. Mr. Ray Kurzweil, to quote the jacket of his book *The Singularity is Near*, is one of the world's leading inventors, thinkers and futurists with a twenty-year track record of accurate predictions. Where will biology be then?

And although Frank Tippler (*Physics of Immortality*) might wish to reduce us to exact copies of ourselves in digital form, I still think that the mystics of the past should be given a chance. Not, I repeat, not religions. Just the mystics, if we ever learn how to decipher the symbolic meaning of their teaching. Until we succeed, we'll probably remain, for the next few million years, as ignorant as we are now. After all, to quote another eminent British broadcaster and science historian James Burke, "evolution advances at somewhere between dead slow and dead slow." Some of us are still fairly primitive. Some of us still seem to enjoy killing just for fun. That second part about killing is my own contribution to the definition of human species. We are killers.

Now I need a dozen imaginary deep bathtubs, with a dozen volunteers, preferably theoretical physicists, who will submerge themselves in the imaginary warm water, relax, and dream up a new universe, which makes sense. The new universe, imaginary or not, would have a reality based on quanta of light. With the incredible diversity of waves at their disposal, they could build our bodies, in their imagination, spanning light-years, or shrinking us to enter and examine an atom from the inside, dodging a cloud of electrons whirling all around us. Wouldn't that be fun?

Just give them a chance. I rather think, that for the theoretical physicist anything is possible, given enough time and enough hot water. Even imaginary time and imaginary water. With the photons, which permeate the whole of even the present universe, imaginary or not, this should be easy.

And the biologists needn't worry. They'll just change their titles to 'photonlogists', and carry on with their selective process of evolution.

Magic, you say? Nah, child's play.

Just wait and see.

And now for a moment of folly, or... a word about electromagnetic spectrum. With the scientists assuring us that the universe consists principally of empty space, let us examine the range of energy that inhabits this abysmal emptiness.

The electromagnetic spectrum is traditionally divided

into regions of radio waves, microwaves, infrared radiation, visible light, ultraviolet rays, x-rays, and gamma rays. The entire range of radiation extending in frequency from approximately 10^{23} hertz to 0 hertz or, in corresponding wavelengths, from 10^{-13} centimeters to infinity and including, in order of decreasing frequency, cosmic-ray photons, gamma rays, x-rays, ultraviolet radiation, visible light, infrared radiation, microwaves, and radio waves. I am offering the abundance of numbers only to illustrate how much more flexibility we would have than we have, at present, with atoms.

Visible light has a wavelength shorter than the size of a bacterium. Radio waves can be as short as a millimeter, or be many, say 30,000, kilometers long. Really! They are very long compared to the rest of the electromagnetic spectrum. The radio spectrum is divided up into a number of 'bands' based on their wavelength and usability for communication purposes. They extend from the Very Low Frequency portion of the spectrum through the Low, Medium, High, Very High, Ultra High, and Super High to the Extra High Frequency range. Above the EHF band comes infrared radiation and *only then* visible light. I think I'd like to have my body constructed from quanta of radio waves. The whole range. Why not? I'd be detectible, and be able to detect my surroundings, for miles, so to speak, as well as squeeze my prongs into very tiny spots.

There are other options, of course. Gamma rays are generated by nuclear reactions (e.g., radioactive decay). At first sight, not much use for those in my photonology, yet, they do exhibit some interesting aspects.

Astronomers have spotted gamma ray emissions coming from the Crab Pulsar at far higher energies than expected. Within the nebula lies the Crab Pulsar—a tiny, rapidly spinning neutron star that sprays highly energetic electromagnetic rays out at its poles like a lighthouse beam, sweeping past the Earth 30 times a second. The pulsar's enormous magnetic field is known to gather up particles and accelerate them—in a process much like particle accelerators here on Earth. As those particles move in curved paths, they emit the gamma rays that we can measure. OK. Maybe we could use some of them. We could give them a spin. Being made up of gamma rays would give us enormous power. The scientists found emissions at more than 100 gigaelectronvolts—100 billion times more energetic than visible light.

Now, that's quite a range of characteristics to choose from. You can confirm some of the data at <http://www.sciencemag.org> and other Internet sources. Some I researched elsewhere. As Shakespeare said, all the world's a stage—my stage. Think of a theater where actors are made up of photons. All sorts of photons. A little like holographic projections, only real.

Why all this data? To stimulate the minds of the theoretical astrophysicists in their bathtubs. Or anyone who takes regular baths.

I will leave you with a poser.

Since we know that neither we, nor the universe is 'solid', and the incredibly diverse spectrum of energy inhabits the whole of the universe, and that energy has characteristics of both, waves and quanta, what if our true nature were to be made up of light? Perhaps it already is, only we can't see most of it.

We could be made up of quanta (not subatomic particles that are essentially empty space, but units or quanta of photons) with wavelength spanning from submicroscopic all the way to infinity. A little like gods. A lot like gods? To quote Sir Isaac Newton, "Are not gross Bodies and Light convertible into one another, ...and may not Bodies receive much of their Activity from the Particles of Light which enter their Composition?"

Was Isaac Newton a scientist or a prophet?

Both, you say?
You may be right!

As for the atheists, it is a matter of unparallel indifference to me whether they are theists, deists, agnostics or atheists. What matters to me is what effect their personal beliefs have on their behaviour and relationship to other people, animals, all living matter and reality in general. There are ample examples of animals acting towards members of *other* species with compassion comparative to that which we, humans, do when seeing our own species in trouble. We tend to ignore those needing our help. Other species don't. Well, those more advanced amongst them. Those not endowed with the selfish gene to the exclusion of all other. Nevertheless, members of various species have been observed helping members of other species, not just those with which they share their a little less-selfish gene.

However, if I understand the evolutionary biologists correctly, they contrive to assign all the goodness, morality, decency, empathy, pity, and of course altruism, exclusively to the "selfish gene", with possible fringe assistance from the memes. They also introduce a concept new to me: that of "reciprocal altruism". Now that's as good an oxymoron as any I've ever heard—although I have heard it said that altruism is not a quality but an act of self-preservation. Nevertheless an act performed with the sole purpose of what one might receive in return, is not altruism at all. It is trade, often selfish, at that.

But to confuse the behaviour known as the Potlatch Effect—wherein one gives only to exhibit one's superiority over the recipient of ones gift—with altruism, as anything by an aberration of ego, is truly a perversion in itself. I am sure there are such humans around, and not just rival chieftains in the Pacific Northwest; but they are as low on the evolutionary scale as a university professor who expects to be accorded respect for having awarded his or her student an undeservedly high mark to raise his own reputation of achievement. Yes, I met such people. Such 'professors'. Edgar Cayce, the late American psychic (a trait dismissed by most biologists), once said that there is only one sin, and that is self. And I suspect he intended the word sin in its original sense, i.e. missing the mark of being human. Or was it of being constructed in the image of god?

Now, I do not object to biologists deifying the gene as the exclusive source of all goodness and altruistic impulses in us, animals, providing they will allot equal measure to our propensity towards murder and mayhem, and to the joy we derive from killing just for fun (as all the hunters will affirm), and to the distinguished scientists who spend half their lives attempting to design and build weapons of mass destruction. I can only assume that the highly altruistic gene is no longer just selfish and, indeed, evolved into a seed of evil, whatever the biologists understand by this word.

I am not sure how such untrammeled biological diversity fits into Pragmatic Realism but, it seems to me, it makes as much sense as being made up of empty space. If so, then the scientists don't really have to make up any of their theories. Perhaps they, too, are filled with empty space—both the scientists and their theories. We seem to make up reality as we go along. Beauty, common sense, even truth, as well as the characteristics of a gene, are in the eyes of the beholder. As for the diverse energies, they continue to exist without our conscious assistance and, after all, as the Preacher in Ecclesiastes 1:1-3, affirms, "There is nothing new under the sun." This same Preacher also proclaims, emphatically, that all actions of man are inherently vain, futile, empty, meaningless, temporary, transitory, fleeting or mere breath. Perhaps we inherited all these traits and abilities from the selfish gene?

On the other hand, the mystics of yore proposed

millennia ago that we are all beings of light. Perhaps their time has come.

Light! Isn't this exactly what String Theory proposes? Does it not affirm that at the fundamental level everything consist of light and electricity? On the other hand, String Theory is already *passé*. What we now have is 5 String Theories. At least we had five, until Edward Witte, an American theoretical physicist compared by many to be today's Einstein, insisted that it's all just One Theory, only we are looking at it from 5 different points of view. And he called it the M Theory. Only no one knows what the M stands for.

You might well ask, "Who cares?"

Well, the scientists are deluding themselves again. Until they'll be able to test the theory, any theory, in a laboratory, even if it's the size of CERN—in part a ring 27 kilometers in circumference and employing some 4000 physicists worldwide—it, the M or any other theory, remains philosophy *not* science.

In the meantime, the scientists at CERN continue to waste our money. They are looking for the Higgs boson which, they say, is a 'fundamental' particle. If we ignore the 'strings' and the ensuing theories, the Higgs boson is expected to be one of the basic building blocks of the Universe. It is also the last missing piece in the leading theory of particle physics—known as the Standard Model—which describes how particles and forces interact. Finding the Higgs was a key goal for the $10bn particle smasher. Now, on the verge of the discovery Prof. Stefan Soldner-Rembold, a senior scientist at CERN had this to say:

"The Higgs particle would, of course, be a great discovery, but it would be an even greater discovery if it didn't exist where theory predicts it to be."

Just think. Something that no one ever saw, touched, smelled, heard, or tasted, with our five senses made up of

mostly empty space, nor detected with the multibillion-dollar technology actually doesn't exist. Wonders will never cease. So much for the $10 billion. Scientists would finally prove that something isn't there. Ain't we got fun?
Back to the drawing board.

On yet another hand, with the exception of the horrendous waste of money, theoretical physicists are much closer to my heart than many other 'all-knowing' scientists. I always said that Einstein was my favourite philosopher. But trust me, at the fundamental level, you and I are just light. And the infinite number of 'strings' all around us is playing an indescribable celestial symphony. Some call it *Musica Universalis*. When you'll hear it—you'll know. God will be the conductor. And then, when you look closer at Maestro's features, you'll recognize your own face.

***

APPENDIX I
The Church

Gleamed from *Essay # 18, Beyond Religion vol. III*,
Dec.7, 2000

Love one another
John 13:34

Sometime ago, a dear friend of mine, having read a number of my essays, suggested that, on occasion, he had an impression that I have it 'in' for the Church. He was very polite about it, but, "Well," he said, "you don't seem to find much good to say about the Holy Mother the Church."

What could I say? I don't.

Not much.

Not as long as the Church, the Holy Roman Catholic and Apostolic Church, takes it upon herself to speak on matters pertaining to the teaching of Christ. For try as I might, each time I attempted to reconcile Christ's teaching with the Church's manifest philosophy, I have been reminded of a man who asked: *"Master, what good thing shall I do, that I may have eternal life?"* And after a preliminary discussion the answer came loud and clear: *"...go and sell that thou hast, and give to the poor, and thou shall have treasure in heaven: and come and follow me."* The last 2000 years made it abundantly clear that the Church has absolutely no interest in any treasures in heaven. On the other hand, the brazen agglomeration of priceless wealth which I suspect exceeds even that of the British Empire, which R. Buckminster Fuller once called: "...history's most successful world-outlaw organization..." leaves me full of admiration. However, since the Church wouldn't follow the Christ, I could hardly be expected to follow the Church.

But this is true *only* of the area of my particular interest. The area of Inquiry into the Nature of Being. Into my personal inquiry into the legacy of past Masters, which to this day appears to remain obscure, enigmatic, full of mystery, to all but few members of the Church I'd ever met.

Perhaps I should meet more people.

On the other hand, I have nothing but admiration and undying gratitude to the Church, present and past, in many other areas that are *almost* as dear to me. I wish my readers, and particularly my friend, to know that I hold the Church responsible for my countless moments of joy, of visual, aural and tactile pleasure that contribute greatly to the fabric of my daily life. In fact, outside my marriage, no other organization contributed so abundantly to the pleasure of my senses as the Church.

Let me count the ways.

I held my breath as I entered the Basilica of Saint Peter. What magnificent space, what resplendent vistas! I dare anyone, of any faith or religion, not to derive pleasure, not to admire the euphoric splendor (spiritual decadence only if you are a spoilsport) of the central building of the Church. The sensuously polished marbles, the forests of columns— forthright and upright, soaring towards heavenly domes, or multihued and spiral, mysterious... filled me with awe. The armies of sculptured saints, the galleries of paintings of more saintly figures, all immortalized right here, on Earth, for posterity. The greatest names of the 16th century, Bramante, Michelangelo and Raphael have been mustered to contribute their genius to this monument of human endeavor. And all this thanks to but one man, Pope Julius II. Admittedly there are those who call his reign "the decadence of papacy", but there is another way of looking at this period. Without Julius, St. Peter would never have happened.

And then there is the Sistine Chapel ceiling, the papal apartments, the papal portrait galleries, the inexhaustible works of art in the Vatican Museum, the consummate splendor of other Vatican buildings, the gardens... and, last but not least, the superb archives of the Vatican library...

Who else could provide us with such unprecedented riches?

And this is just the headquarters.

Wherever I went, wherever I have traveled, in Europe, in Africa, in the North, Central or South America, everywhere, in every country, my joy was multiplied by the sheer numbers of beautiful churches, often amassing the best art and architecture that money could buy of local and imported talent. Often of genius left unknown, forgotten in small Brazilian, Mexican, Peruvian towns, in neglected English villages, in small hamlets the world over. The Gothic style alone could not have been inspired by any authority other than that of the Church. The Early English, the Decorated, the Curvilinear or Flamboyant, the sedate more reserved Tudor, all testify to the Church reaching ever higher, yet ever more lugubriously, for something she, the church, seems to have lost. But for me, for my own pleasure, the heritage speaks of nothing but beauty, of human endeavor, of the creative spirit.

And then, by unmitigated contrast I saw the inspiring, flowing, soaring effects of Amiens and other ecclesiastic monuments of the great French Cathedral cities... high towers, pinnacles, superabundant sculpture, effervescent stained glass, filtering preternatural light to the streamlined interiors. Wherever the Church stretched her mighty arms, she left an indelible mark of beauty in her prodigious wake.

And then there is music.

I defy anyone to point to any other source as abundant as the Church in commanding composers to produce their best for the good of all. Music cannot be retained by those who commissioned its fervor. It is a free gift to all that would listen. From the *aria antiqua*, through the doleful canticles to the Ambrosian and Gregorian chants, echoing among the stone walls of ancient monasteries, to Handel's Messiah and other Oratorios. And who could claim that Bach wasn't first and foremost a church's composer? And then we find Tosca's incomparable *Vissi d'arte*, Desdemona's plaintive *Ave Maria*, Elizabeth de Valois's *Tu che le vanita conoscesti* and so many other sublime arias all, surely, inspired by the Church's teaching. And finally there is Mozart who, through his ecstatic prodigious and ebullient *Requiem,* allowed us a peak into his personal heaven. Could any of these have been born without the Church's influence?

I think not.

And there is more—much more...

So I am to this day, and intend to remain, grateful to the Holy Mother, the Church. Grateful for her past inspiration and for giving access to us all, today, to share in her splendid, unequal aegis. And to those who belittle her wealth, I can only ask: Who else is prepared to spend millions, countless millions, on the maintenance of such legacy?

Perhaps this fact alone is the greatest blessing. The Church is assuring that the wonder of human creativity will remain accessible not only to us but also to our children's children. Who says the Church cannot serve two masters?

Perhaps we should forgive and forget the preacher's peccadilloes and be grateful for his obvious achievements. By standing on guard of such illustrious past, perhaps the Church might also inspire our distant future.

And, after all, the future is our own.

***

APPENDIX II
Science

*"It is important to foster individuality
for only the individual can produce the new ideas."*

Albert Einstein

Even as I felt the need to express my gratitude to the administrators of the Church of Rome, I likewise feel the same sentiment towards a great many scientists, who spent their lives, if on occasion unwittingly, in an extended attempt to improve the quality of my life.

Whether it was first said by Samuel Johnson, John Ray, or Saint Bernard of Clairvaux, the fact remains that hell, or the road to hell, is paved with good intentions. Nevertheless, while many a positive event happens unintentionally, a useful prerequisite for positive results is the motivating intention. A man whose intention is to saves lives, seldom kills. Thus a surgeon seldom kills, while a soldier does so more often. A scientist whose intention is to produce the best in technology is likely to enhance our lives, while one who's only purpose is to make money will end up a parasite, even if he, ultimately, (moved by genetically implanted pangs of conscience?) gives away a portion of his fortune later. A research biologist working to produce a life-saving serum will seldom produce poison.

Yes, intention does matter, but it cannot be used as an excuse. Let us examine the issue from the perspective of Pragmatic Realism.

Imagine a world in which the air is pure. There would hardly be any lung diseases, reducing substantially the cost of Medicare. The savings in cost could be transferred to insulate residential homes better, eliminating the need for expensive heating, and the attendant pollution. In turn, the money saved could be invested into healthier food products, resulting in a healthier population, which would again result in less money being spent on medical treatment. Perhaps then medicine would concentrate on prophylactic solutions rather than on treating the pathological results of others' ignorance. Imagine a world in which scientists are not so corrupt as to flood the market of ignorant masses with tobacco. (Imperial Tobacco Group PLC announced: "Our current *scientific* programmes are undertaken to *improve* our knowledge of *tobacco* and *smoking...*").

The story goes on.

The same could be said of scientists who concern themselves with human comfort.

Industrial revolution raised the standard of living for millions of people, but it also produced unprecedented amount of waste, of which air pollution is only a part. Is it the fault of the inventor or the user? Can scientists be blamed for enabling people to travel in equally unprecedented comfort, be it in cars or in airplanes? Yes, they aught to know better. After all they claim to know better. If their primary purpose, their intention, had been to transport people while causing an absolute minimum of noise, smell, poisonous particles suspended in the air we breathe, than the consequences of their efforts would be very noticeable today. If they simply carried out the orders of their 'superiors', of people whose sole intention was to make money, regardless of the consequences, then they, the scientist and engineers do participate in the guilt.

So what am I grateful for?

First and foremost by igniting the holly fire of curiosity in all who feel the need to examine the reality we live in. The technology they invented enables me to speak to friends who are far away from the comfort of my well insulated, water and fire-resistant house.

All in all, I am grateful for the ease of life with which the scientists have surrounded me. I am grateful for all discoveries, which enhanced my concept of Pragmatic Reality in which I experience my becoming.

There are many, many things I am grateful for.

Thank you, scientists. May your comfort level be as pleasant as mine is. I hope you'll continue to enhance life here, on Earth, without reaching out to the Moon, or Mars. If you do reach out, let it be, for instance, to conquer gravity, rather by expelling tons of pollutants into the atmosphere in your attempt to fight it. Please, act like scientists, not like henchman of pollsters and politicians. Let them stew in their own quagmire. Unless… unless you want to sent them all to the moon… soon?

Well…

Now, a word about scientists at their best.

On November 18, 2011 the BBC Internet News reported the unveiling by the US engineers the "World's lightest material." The Engineers say the material is less dense than aerogels and metallic foams.

> "The substance is said to be made out of tiny hollow metallic tubes arranged into a micro-lattice—a crisscrossing diagonal pattern with small open spaces between the tubes." The researchers say the material is 100 times lighter than Styrofoam and has 'extraordinarily high energy absorption' properties. Potential uses include next-generation batteries and shock absorbers."

The research was carried out at the University of California, Irvine, HRL Laboratories and the California Institute of Technology, and is published in the latest edition of Science.

"The trick is to fabricate a lattice of interconnected hollow tubes with a wall thickness 1,000 times thinner than a human hair," said lead author of the announcement, Dr Tobias Schaedler.

The resulting material has a density of 0.9 milligrams per cubic centimeter.

"By comparison the density of silica aerogels—the world's lightest solid materials—is only as low as 1.0mg per cubic cm. The metallic micro-lattices have the edge because they consist of 99.99% air and of 0.01% solids."

"Materials actually get stronger as the dimensions are reduced to the nanoscale," said team member Lorenzo Valdevit. "Combine this with the possibility of tailoring the architecture of the micro-lattice and you have a unique cellular material."

The engineers suggest that practical uses for the substance include thermal insulation, battery electrodes and products that need to dampen sound, vibration and shock energy.

(The whole article was gleamed from the BBC mobile News Technology. The rest of the article can be read at:
http://www.bbc.co.uk/news/technology-15788735).

Before I took up writing, I'd spend many years designing buildings. I would have given a great deal to have such a material at my disposal. My congratulations to the US engineers, to all the scientists involved, and to BBC who were kind enough to make the information available to us.

Now if you accept that the "metallic micro-lattices have the edge because they consist of 99.99% air", and multiply the result by 99.9999999999999% void in every atom of which the lattice is made, you get some idea of what I mean when I say that the world you experience with your senses is not real.

***

APPENDIX III
Richard Dawkins

"Let us try to teach generosity and altruism, because we are born selfish."

Clinton Richard Dawkins, DSc, FRS, FRSL, ethologist, evolutionary biologist, and writer.

Finally a word about the man, who not only is my favorite biologist, but is the scientist who also inspired this book. My admiration for Richard Dawkins and his brilliant mind has waned somewhat following his persistent attacks not on religions, in which endeavour he has my full support, but at his juvenile and pathetic repeated commentaries on biblical stories of which he understands absolutely nothing.

While mentioning that he is aware of other, non-literal explanations of the scriptures, nonetheless he continued to repeat, time after time, his pitiable fundamentalist versions, which can only serve to discourage others from even attempting to understand what is evidently beyond Dawkins's scope, and simply to dismiss all the scriptures as dismal nonsense. One can but wonder why his opposition, those who disagree with him, use equally as inane arguments, as those of e.g. Pat Robertson, quoted by him. Action equals equal and opposite reaction: nonsense to nonsense. I tend to think that the author deludes himself if he imagines that he converted a single reader to his way of thinking. Pity. I'd venture to suggest that he is endowed by the selfish gene with a superb brain, which, outside the domain of biology, he fails to put to good use.

Although my learned hero claims that some people in America, having read his books, had given up their religions, such people, I suspect, were already well advanced into their apostate state of mind. Those deeply rooted in their religions, however, will only have an equal and opposite reaction. The email Dawkins quotes from a young medical student, who having renounced faith lost his girlfriend, is a perfect example of this. Hatred is said to breed hatred. Love seems to attract love. Both these adages seem to suggest very pragmatic solutions.

However, I am prepared to forgive all scientists a great deal for one reason alone. They often feel so passionately about science that I am sure they're in love with it. And we all know that love is blind. And as I am told that most scientists are atheists and monists (in the material sense of the word) the rest of my notes will address scientists in general.

It seems that evolution equipped scientists' brains to navigate a world that to them is real, and thus assures their survival. It is a world based 100% on material reality, guided by physical, or sensory observations, of things past. We must never forget that whatever we examine in physical world, that object is substantially if not completely changed at cellular and/or atomic level, before the examination is completed. This is a 'scientific' fact.

My world is one in which I continuously find themes to explore which are not necessary for my physical survival. Some great, great men lived a very short time (see Chapter 19). In my world the survival of my imagination, my emotions, my mind, of that which inspires me to feel, to recognize poetry and beauty in literature, music, dance and all forms of art, is of vastly more importance. During and immediately after WW2, I met people who were physically very much alive, but they lost the capacity to love. This symptom, it seems, is repeated by the veterans of each and every war. They are the living dead, regardless what biology tells us about them. I dare suggest, that it is much easier for me to understand the world of the scientists than for them to understand mine. I don't mean the intricacies of quantum mechanics. I mean that their world is only real if it can be objectively shared, if we all perceive reality in exactly the same way.

My world is filled with individuality, uniqueness, subjectivity, delight and euphoric appreciations of beauty in the eyes of the beholder. Even just a single beholder. The scientists will argue that you can do none of these things if you are physically dead. My response is that if you don't do at least some of these things, you already are dead.

Scientists' problem seems to be that most of them, recognize only material objects as real. If I close my eyes and see the image of my wife, that image is for me, just as real. If I dream and learn to enter and control the passage of my dream (known as lucid dreaming), even if I only think I did so, the events, pleasure, joys, beauty, even scents and tactile pleasure within my dream, are all just as real. My reality is not confined to the mundane sensory input. Perhaps it was evolution which equipped me with the capacity to experience my dreams with all my senses, but how can anyone deny my reality if they've never experienced it? Can a blind man deny the sight others enjoy? Perhaps if he was born blind, but what if he, the scientist, decided to pluck out his own eyes, as so many scientists do? None are so blind as those who have eyes yet cannot see...

We must be careful. Perhaps evolution leaves behind those who are anchored too much in the past. Or in a material reality at the expense of all others.

Science, to repeat, examines only that which is, or more accurately, that which was. Poets and artists live in a different world that opens its doors to realities scientists have never dreamt of. Sadly, most of them never will.

I, for one, try to refrain from offering explanations of stories in the Bible, other than those few in my *Dictionary of Biblical Symbolism*, which I included for the sole purpose of illustrating how the Dictionary *might* be used. I am sure there are other sources. I am also of the opinion that each one of us reaches a certain stage in the evolution of our consciousness at which time he or she begins knocking at the door of knowledge sequestered within the depth of our unconscious. When that time comes, providing we learn how the key works, we all find our own explanations. At that time we also find the key to our, individual, immortality.

After all, to repeat once again the wisdom gained by Carl G. Jung, individual is the only reality.

I agree with Dawkins's comments regarding the consequences of *Zeitgeist*.

[Wikipedia offers this definition of the word: *Zeitgeist* is the general, cultural, intellectual, ethical, spiritual or political climate within a nation or even specific groups, along with the general ambiance, morals, socio-cultural direction, and mood associated with an era].

There appears to be a small group of people, which is head and shoulders above the masses. I call this elite "the chosen few". To make sure that I am not misinterpreted, let me assure everyone that we and we alone do the 'choosing'. Usually it is the consequence of sublimating one's ego and erasing that invisible barrier between 'us' and 'them'.

The state of consciousness of those few, however, or their state of advancement, has little to do with whether they were, or are, religious or not. If religion's job is to reconnect us with our own potential, than, having done so, religion has already done its job. Regrettably, few people seem aware of this.

I find it amusing to note, however, that while my illustrious author confesses to being an "amateur (in) psychology and sociology" which inadequacy is stopping him from explaining why "moral Zeitgeist moves in its concentrated way," the same lack of expertise has no restraining influence on his oozing venom on the Bible. And this although he claims that he does not, "by nature, strive on confrontation." Nevertheless, he goes a long way to prove that he has no idea what the Bible's inner or esoteric meaning is. He also gives an impression that he has absolutely no idea what most people mean by the word 'god'—which is hardly surprising considering I never met two men, or women, who shared the same meaning. On the other hand, had I limited myself to writing books exclusively on architecture, I wouldn't have written 30 books on a variety of subjects.

One can only wonder, as apparently he does, how he "acquired a reputation for pugnacity towards religion". I respectfully suggest, that if he really wants to know, he should read a little book *he* wrote about *Delusion*.

I also beg to differ with people who place most wars squarely on the shoulders of religion. Although at first sight it may seem so, the common atheists' contention that wars are initiated in the name of religions or religious dogmas, is false. There are many leaders, presidents, prime ministers or Führers, if you will, who *use* religious beliefs to mobilize simple minds (I am sorry to say that is the overwhelming majority) to wage wars, almost invariably for *economic* reasons. They use people under whatever pretext is available to advance their own end. Religions are the means, not the reason.

This in no way detracts from Dawkins's frightening and to my mind accurate description of the power that 'religious faith' has on the young minds of the aspiring Islamic martyrs. It is the same power, which had enabled Christians to reaffirm their faith while facing lions in the Coliseum in Rome. Wouldn't it be nice if we learned to ignite the same fire for, perhaps, more pacifistic ends? For ends in which not only the 'martyr' is the sole 'beneficiary' (speedy arrival in Paradise) of their sacrifice? Perhaps, only when we forsake our concern for our physical bodies, and reject the fear of death, that we shall be able to rise to those incredible heights and sink to such abysmal depths. Regrettably, natural selection cannot help us with that.

And then there is his impassioned attack on faith itself.

His are passions, quite understandably, fuelled by terrorist attacks, motivated by misinterpretation of religious writing. But let's face it, any man whose concept of 'heaven', let alone immortality, is defined by 72 virgins, cannot be in full command of his senses. Even basic logic would tell one that 72 virgins wouldn't last that long, and one, alas, is supposed to remain in Paradise for ever and ever. Are the virgins renewable? It is not faith we should combat, but insanity, ignorance and mental retardation.

It is plainly evident that no self-immolator ever read the scriptures he claims to have followed. Furthermore, let us not forget that the Qur'an, or Koran, teaches that Islam is the continued faithful religion in the same line as the Prophets who came before Muhammad: *The same religion has He established for you as that which He enjoined on Noah ... and that which We enjoined on Abraham, Moses, and Jesus* (42:13 AYA).

In the Old and New Testaments we are told not to kill, and even to love our enemy. Where does the murder and lack of tolerance originate? I suggest, again, it has its roots not with any of the scriptures but, as and since the days of the crusades, it originates with the rabbis and priests and imams. Perhaps all that is needed is sequestering any and all teachers or interpreters of any religious scriptures who advocate any violence whatsoever.

That still leaves us with purely secular misfits who go under very different names. But whatever the evil of 9/11 or the London Underground or Madrid bombings, or any of the religiously inspired murders, none can aspire to equal the purely secular, dare I say 'dispassionately atheistic', wholesale murder of Hiroshima and Nagasaki, or even the estimated 22,000 victims Katyń, for that matter. Let the black pans leave the kettles alone.

The Doctor quotes in his book, the case of Kurt Wise, a man who obtained higher degrees in geology and paleontology only to reject his learning in preference of fundamentalist interpretation of the Bible, is doubly sad. Not only because Kurt Wise devolved intellectually in favour of emotional satisfaction (and perhaps fear), but because others, who should know better, did not make the slightest effort to show him that there is absolutely no contradiction between the Biblical and 'scientific' teaching.

And, by the way, the theologians' symbolical or allegorical interpretations of the Bible have little to do with what I am advocating. I did not study the Bible to prove anything. I merely wanted to find out, what it's about. If it is such nonsense as atheists insists, then how come it survived, in one form or another, in spite of many divergent translations, for some 2000 years? Well, now I know and he, Kurt Wise, still doesn't.

What a pity...

To do it 'my way', one must start with an open mind. If one was a 'believer', one has to go through a period of apostasy. To be able to pour "new wine into old bottles", one must clean them really well. Otherwise, like Kurt Wise, one will suffer from dichotomy. One can be attached to an idea with love or with hatred—with equal force. As I have mentioned above a number of times, belief and Gnosticism or knowledge deal with completely different subjects. They are stimulated by different motivations. Alas, the fundamentalist scientists are as stubborn in their ways, as religious are in theirs. To both of them the Bible remains a delusion.

Regrettably, trying to explain spiritual knowledge (reality, evolution, immortality, etc.) to a confirmed scientific fundamentalist is like trying to discuss the intricacies of Beethoven's Fifth with a man born deaf. He'll never believe that Beethoven's ears were filled with music even after he suffered from tinnitus.

As for atheists, here's a final word to all who misinterpret the Bible. The expression: "Ye are gods", in Hebrew, means: "You are objects of worship". The same Hebrew word is used to describe the 'objects' that created the world in Genesis 1:1. Think about it. Until I saw the same word used in Psalm 82:6, I suspected that the ancients may have been referring to non-biological creatures of some sort, and thus referred to them as "objects of worship". Or… they still could have been hoping that, one day, we might become as clever and as powerful as those original "objects of worship" which (who?) 'created' the world, and set the evolution going. Of course, according to Ray Kurzweil, we would be represented by robots worthy of worship.

And what of Pragmatic Reality?

I'd rather be a Buddhist. At least, like Moses and Yeshûa (see Chapter 14), at the risk of uttering blasphemy, I could be a god, if I wanted to be one. I understand that people are no longer crucified for having such beliefs, although I am told that in some parts of the world one could still lose one's head. Remind me not to travel too far.

I will let you go with just two more quotes from my favourite scientist, Albert Einstein. The first is a comment on Pragmatic Realism; the second, on my personal philosophy of life.

"Reality is merely an illusion, albeit a very persistent one."

"A person starts to live when he can live outside himself."

***

EPILOGUE

*"If you suspect you are more than flesh and bones, read Stan I.S. Law.
If you want to be sure, read Stanislaw Kapuscinski."*

(Anonymous email received by the author)

My brother came to see me, today. We discussed this and that, and later, since he has a Ph.D. in physics from Leeds, UK, our conversation turned to physics. Particle physics, or as I like call it, non-pragmatic reality.

I told him about the empty space business. About our reality not being there. Or here, so to speak. I was hoping he'd cheer me up.

He didn't.

He said that the latest coming directly from the hot tub is nothing. I mean that atoms occupy, well, zero space. That, according to the particle physicists, they are points. Non-dimensional points. They are called point-particles. That atoms are there but not really, as far as mass is concerned.

No mass?

Not in particle physics. It's useful, he said. They don't take up any space. It's how physicists see the particles when mass is, well, mass and size or shape, or... structure is irrelevant in a given context...

So they are not really there?

Oh, they are there. Sort of.

What about the Earth, I asked? Is Earth a point, too?
Sure, he replied.
And the universe?
He just looked at me.
So much for Pragmatic Reality of particle physics.
Then I tried again. What about the Big Bang, then? It must have had an enormous black hole to initiate the expansion of the whole universe. The mass of our own black hole, at the center of Milky Way, is said to be about four million times that of our Sun. And our little solar system is only some 27,000 light-years away from the centre of the Milky Way—from the mother of all the black holes in our galaxy. I wondered how long it would or how long it will take to swallow us whole.
A point, he replied. A point.
You're kidding, right?
No. Particle physicists never kid. Science is too vital. The whole reality would collapse if we did. Wouldn't it? I must have looked dubious. You see, he added, before the Big Bang there was no time or space. Hence…
A point, I finished for him.
I must have continued to look a bit lost.
You see, he began again, for example, from far enough away an object of any shape will look and behave as a point-like object.
This time it was I who just stared at him. He continued talking. In the theory of gravity, we often discuss a point mass, meaning a point particle with a nonzero mass and…
I stopped paying attention.
My wife looked up from the settee. I'd rather be a fish, she said. When we both looked at her, she added, but not salmon.
Yesterday we saw a movie on TV about salmon. They, seemingly hundreds of them, have reached the end of their journey. Three brown bears were gorging themselves in shallow water. The salmon made only half-hearted attempt at

escape. What would have been the point? They came here to die.

It's all a delusion, I thought. Like God?

I thought that Dr. Dawkins would be pleased. On the other hand, the non-physical universe of spiritual, mental and emotional whimsy suddenly became even more real. At least for me. How about you?

***

BIBLIOGAPHY

Arnold, Sir Edwin, M.A., K.C.I.E., C.S.I., *The Song Celestial or Bhagavad Gita,* (Self-Realization Fellowship, LA.).
Black, Margaret J. *Freud and Beyond* (Harper Collins)
Blavatsky, H.P., (And Abridgement of) *The Secret Doctrine*, (The Theosophical Publishing House).
Green, Brian, *The Elegant Universe*, (Vintage Books, Random House, Inc. New York).
Campbell, Joseph, *The Hero with a Thousand Faces*, (Bollingen Series XVII, Princeton University Press).
Dawkins, Richard, *Climbing Mount Improbable,* (W.W. Norton & Co., New York, London)
Dawkins, Richard, *The God Delusion,* (Houghton Mifflin Harcourt)
Fouts, Roger and Tukel Mills, Stephen, *Next of Kin: My conversations with Chimpanzees,* (William Morrow Paperbacks)
Hacker, Randi, *Close Call 1: Survival of the Fittist,* ebook, (Smashwords Edition).
Imperial Reference Bible, King James Version, (Thomas Nelson Inc.).
Kapuscinski, Stanislaw, *Beyond Religion I, Essay #52,* ebook, Inhousepress, (Amazon/Kindle and Smashwords).
Kapuscinski, Stanislaw, *Beyond Religion II, Fundamentalism, Spirit,* ebook, Inhousepress, (Amazon/Kindle and Smashwords).
Kapuscinski, Stanislaw, *Beyond Religion III, The Green Eyed Monster, Church,* ebook, Inhousepress, (Amazon/Kindle and Smashwords).
Kapuscinski, Stanislaw, *Key to Immortality;* Commentary on the Gospel of Thomas, ebook, Inhousepress, (Amazon/Kindle and Smashwords).
Kapuscinski, Stanislaw, *Dictionary of Biblical Symbolism,* ebook, Inhousepress, (Amazon/Kindle and Smashwords).
Krishnamurti, J., *Exploration into Insight*, (Harper & Row).
Jayakar Pupul, *Krishnamurti*, a biography, (Harper & Row).
Kurzweil, Ray, *The Singularity is Near*, (Viking, Penguin Group).
Lao-Tzu, *Tao Te Ching*, Transl. by D. Lau, (Alfred A. Knopf).
Lederman, Leon, with Teresi, Dick, *The God Particle*, (Houghton Mifflin Company).

Monahan, Evelyn, M., *The Miracle of Metaphysical Healing*, (Prentice Hall Trade).
Pearson, Carol S. Ph.D., *The Hero Within*, (Harper Collins).
Prabhupada, A.C. Bhaktivedanta Swami, *Bhagavad-Gita, As It Is*, (The Bhaktivedanta Book Trust).
The Nag Hammadi Library, The definitive new translation of the Gnostic scriptures, James M. Robinson, General Editor, (Harper San Francisco).
Tippler, Franks, *Physics of Immortality*, (Anchor Books, Doubleday).
Twitchell, Paul, *Shariyat-Ki-Sugmad*, Illuminated Wary Press.
Venter, J. Craig, *A Life Decoded*, (Penguin Books).
Waldrop, M. Mitchell, *Complexity—The Emerging science at the edge of Order and Chaos*, (Touchstone Book, Simon & Shuster).
Watson, Lyall, *Lightning Bird,* (Hodder and Stoughton Ltd, Coronet edition).

Acknowledgments

I would be remiss were I not to thank my many friends for their comments, advice, and proofreading, none more so than Ronald Piecuch who's editing raised to book to acceptable literary standards. As always my gratitude to my wife, Bozena Happach, who put up with being a grass widow for weeks on end, and then offered me her inspired insights.

Sincerely,
Stanisław Kapuściński

Smashwords wrote in their Annual Review:

If you write a book that touches your readers' soul, or inspires them with passion or knowledge, your readers will market your book for you.

I've done my part. The rest is up to you.
And if you enjoyed my efforts, please write a (brief) review.
Your thoughts are important to me.

A Word about the Author

Stanislaw Kapuscinski, (aka **Stan I.S. Law**), architect, sculptor and prolific writer was educated in Poland and England. Since 1965 he has resided in Canada. His special interests cover a broad spectrum of arts, sciences and philosophy. His fiction and non-fiction attest to his particular passion for the scope and the development of human potential. He authored more than thirty books, nineteen of them novels.

Under his real name he published seven non-fiction books sharing his vision of reality. He also composed two collections of poems in his original native tongue in which he satirizes his view of the world while paying homage to Bozena Happach's sculptures.

Finally, he and his wife publish two blogs online, which, to date of this printing have been visited by hundreds of thousands of people. We both hope you'll enjoy them as much.

*****
62,627

VISUALIZATION

CREATING YOUR OWN UNIVERSE

Stanisław Kapuściński

THIS BOOK WILL HELP YOU STAND ON YOUR OWN FEET
WITH SUCH CONFIDENCE THAT NOTHING WILL EVER UPSET
YOUR BALANCE

INHOUSEPRESS, MONTREAL, CANADA
http://inhousepress.ca

www.ingramcontent.com/pod-product-compliance
Lightning Source LLC
Chambersburg PA
CBHW022355040426
42450CB00005B/196